RESTORATION AND REPAIR
A Handbook for Use at Home

Michèle Brown was educated at St. Anne's College, Oxford, and has a degree in Modern History. For several years she worked as a presenter/reporter for both BBC and ITV and has talked about restoring furniture on many programmes including BBC radio's Woman's Hour and Thames Television's Good Afternoon. She has had her own column in *Living Magazine*, and as well as writing about the subject she also gives lectures about collecting and caring for antiques. Her other books include *Queen Elizabeth II – The Silver Jubilee Book*, *The Little Royal Book*, *Food by Appointment* and *Restoring Old Junk*.

TEACH YOURSELF BOOKS

RESTORATION AND REPAIR

A Handbook for Use at Home

Michèle Brown

Illustrations by
David Farris

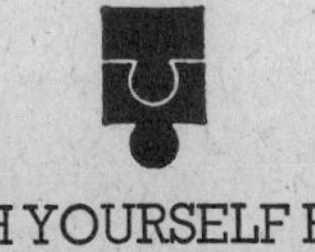

TEACH YOURSELF BOOKS
Hodder and Stoughton

First impression 1978

ISBN 0 340 22850 4

Printed and bound in Great Britain for Hodder and Stoughton Paperbacks, a division of Hodder and Stoughton Ltd, Mill Road, Dunton Green, Sevenoaks, Kent (Editorial Office: 47 Bedford Square, London WC1 3DP) by Hazell Watson & Viney Ltd, Aylesbury, Bucks

Contents

Introduction

This book is to help you care for, and repair where necessary, all those things which together furnish your home: furniture, pictures and picture frames, china and glass, books. It deals with running repairs on minor areas of damage, such as heat stains on wood. It also shows you how to undertake more major tasks, such as reseating a caned chair. Often it is hard to tell from the description of a repairing technique just how difficult it is in practice. The size of the job is not really a guide—stripping and revarnishing a large table is uncomplicated, while replacing a small patch of veneer is extremely difficult. I have therefore indicated where a technique is too advanced for even the most adept novice, especially where the instructions are deceptively simple.

Although the book is divided into basic chapters, the sections within those chapters are clearly defined, so that if you want to deal with an isolated problem, such as replacing castors, you can go straight to it without having to read the entire chapter. There is a whole section on materials needing special care such as marble and alabaster. Additional useful information which may come under another section is cross-referenced. There is a full index to enable you to go straight to the section of the book which is most relevant to you. There are short chapters on the applications of solvents and on how to remove everyday stains. These will probably have a more general use than the subject of this book. There is a limited book list for those who might like to take a particular branch of restoration to a more specialist level. If this book arouses your interest in a specialist field you will undoubtedly be able to find a complete book on that subject through your local library or bookshop.

I

What to look for and where to find it

One reason for learning the basic techniques of restoring furniture is that they will enable you to repair furniture you already own which has become damaged or which has started to look a little less attractive than it used to. The other reason is that you can then buy secondhand furniture, which is often more interesting and attractive than modern mass-produced furniture, and be confident that you have the know-how to put right any imperfections. If you can do the work yourself you are far more likely to come across a bargain: once the seller has paid a professional to put the faults right he puts up the price accordingly.

If you are looking for furniture in this category you will be fortunate indeed if you find high quality antiques which have gone unnoticed by buyers who are in the antique trade. In fact, it is really better to avoid very high class furniture which is damaged unless it is extremely cheap. This is because the best thing to do with it is to take it to a professional restorer rather than risk ruining it further yourself, and professional restorers are expensive. You can furnish a home relatively cheaply, attractively and interestingly if you look out for the sort of items shown in the illustrations. These are old enough not to depreciate as soon as you have bought them and sturdy enough to take a little rough treatment when you start trying out your repairing and restoring techniques.

It is becoming harder all the time to find furniture at real bargain prices, now that so many people are looking for the same things, but there are still some places which offer more chances than others; junk shops which are really dusty and dirty for example, but not the type where items are artlessly arranged to look as if you might find something interesting and where every item has a code and not a price stuck onto it. This code usually means that the seller charges

DIAGRAM I

what he thinks you will pay. One good source of furniture is the 'For Sale' column of a local newspaper, as long as you are able to transport your purchase home yourself. Street markets are also good places, especially those in the less 'touristy' parts of the country. If the town is not large enough to have a guide to that type of facility, ring up the local council or local traders' association to find out when and where the market is held.

Auctions are probably the best place of all for finding what you want at the price you want to pay. If you are not used to auctions it is a good idea to go along to a few simply as an observer before you start to bid at one. You will probably find that real collector's items fetch very high prices from the dealers, but items which are not of such high quality are very cheap. Getting good value at an auction is often just a matter of luck. Country house auctions seem to fetch higher prices than sales of miscellaneous items from more than one source. In the summer when many dealers are on holiday the prices may not get pushed as high as usual, and bad weather may prevent people going to an auction and thus keep prices down. A lot of fuss is made about the difficulties of bidding and of the dangers of coming home with a stuffed bear or something equally outrageous simply because you scratched your nose at the wrong time. Although regular bidders at large salerooms may have a recognised signal for the auctioneer which prevents rivals from knowing who else is bidding for the same lot, the procedure is generally much more straightforward. It is best simply to call out clearly and distinctly what you wish to

DIAGRAM 2

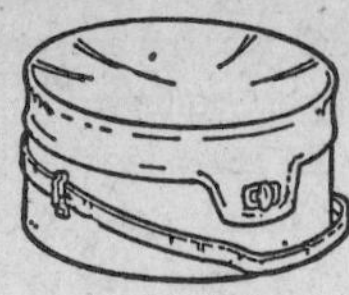

DIAGRAM 3

bid. It is even becoming less usual for an auctioneer to call out 'Going, going, gone'. Instead he will probably ask whether anyone wants to make an increase on the last bid.

Magazines about antiques, as well as newspapers, give details of forthcoming auctions. Local salerooms usually have one regular day a week when they hold an auction. There is almost always a preview day when you can inspect the goods. Get a catalogue and go to the preview. You should always thoroughly inspect any item you are considering making a bid for. If there is a 'lot' listed which you cannot find, ask to see it; it has probably been locked away for safe keeping because it is fragile. Remember to look at the back and underneath of furniture, where you are most likely to detect problems such as woodworm.

When you have decided what you want to bid for, mark it in the catalogue along with the price you are prepared to pay for it. Mark a realistic price, not one which just sounds like a neat round figure. Do not be surprised if a dealer drops out before you do. This does not necessarily mean that you are over-paying; the dealer will have to add his own mark-up when he resells the item, and this could make it too expensive for a potential customer. Do not allow yourself to get carried away and pay more than the price you have marked. On the other hand it is worth remembering that items such as occasional tables are very popular and you will therefore have to pay relatively more than you would for a large item such as a mahogany wardrobe.

If you do want a large item bear in mind that you are responsible for transporting it away from the sale. If you have to pay a removal firm to do this for you, include the price in your estimate of what it is worth to you. If you have not arranged transport immediately you will probably have to pay storage charges until you collect your purchase. All goods have to be paid for before they are collected.

Although you are unlikely to be buying and restoring top quality antiques it is a good idea to know as much as possible about the best available, so that you know what to look for. A good way to do this is to familiarise yourself with museum collections—no amount of description in a book can equal the sight of the real thing. There are several monthly magazines dealing with antique or near-antique furniture, and year books are available which are packed with information. These are generally kept by libraries if you do not want the annual expense of buying them yourself. Libraries also usually keep price guides which are another useful type of annual publication. These have illustrations of typical items with an indication of the type of price they are fetching. The prices always tend to be a little on the low side as they are intended for dealers and are based on the previous year's prices. As well as these books there are many small pocket books on particular subjects which are useful to carry with you if you are collecting one particular type of item. For example, if you are interested in pewter it is a good idea to carry around with you one of the several small handbooks available which list pewter touch marks. You will then be able to check the age and origin of any piece you come across. Similar books are available for silver and gold hallmarks and china marks.

2

Tools and equipment

It pays in the long run to buy good quality tools if you intend to do much furniture restoration. The best approach is to buy what you need as you go along, so that if you find your real interest and skill is for repairing china, you have not wasted money on expensive specialist tools for woodwork. If you already have a workbench you will be equipped with items such as a block plane. This and similar items are not included in this list, which is intended only to cover the very basic hand tools required by people who do not want to buy a comprehensive workbench straightaway. With these tools you will be able to manage a wide variety of basic techniques with the minimum outlay. More specialist items of equipment are mentioned under the various topics covered.

Keep tools in good condition and make sure all cutting tools are kept sharp for maximum efficiency and safety.

Panel saw with flexible blade for rough sawing
Tenon saw (small) for fine sawing
Hand drill
Drill bits (various sizes)
Hammer (medium weight) for hammering nails
Tack hammer for upholstery and delicate work
Wooden mallet (small) for working directly on wood and dowelling
Screwdrivers (medium and small)
Old large screwdriver for odd jobs, *e.g.* as makeshift chisel
Bradawl (small) for making small holes
Pliers
Stanley knife and blades
Assorted nails and screws
Woodworker's adhesive
Epoxy adhesive

Paint stripper
Paint brushes (see p. 48ff)
Methylated spirit
White spirit (turpentine substitute)
Steel wool (medium and fine grade)
Abrasive paper (assorted grades)
Wet and dry paper for delicate work
Plastic wood for filling holes and cracks in wood and other materials
Clean, lint-free rags such as old handkerchiefs
Vice (portable, multi-purpose)—essential for holding things firmly while you are working with sharp tools
Rubber gloves
Disposable plastic gloves
Overall
Piece of old PVC flooring material to protect work surface while using tools
Lock-up cupboard for dangerous equipment and chemicals

A fundamental kit, condensed from this list, is shown in the illustration.

A Panel saw
B Vice
C Bradawl
D Stanley knife
E Mallet
F Hammer
G Tenon saw
H Screwdriver

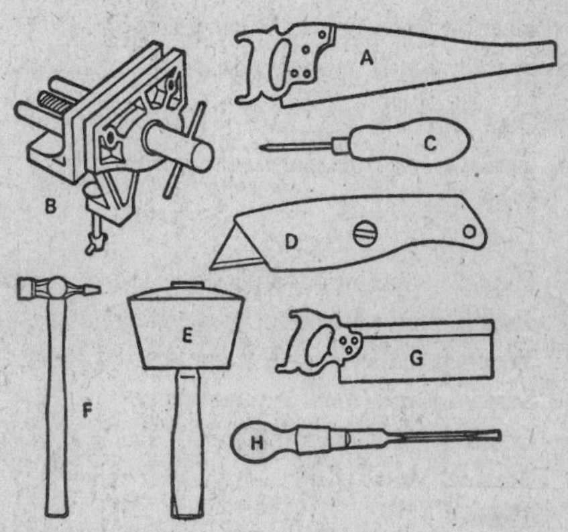

3

Repairing wooden furniture

Simple repairs for burns, cracks, scratches etc. on wood

Heat marks (white stains)

On polished wood rub over the area with methylated spirit on a clean, lint-free rag. This will clean off the finish and may in itself darken the wood a little to match the surrounding finish. When the methylated spirit has dried, apply a little wax shoe polish to the affected area: a light, medium or dark tan will usually provide a good match. Apply this polish sparingly and build up several layers of a lighter colour rather than risk spoiling the colour match with one heavy application of a dark colour. When this coloured polish has been rubbed into the wood you can repolish the whole surface with a good quality white wax furniture polish. It will do no harm to use the methylated spirit on a wider area than the patch affected by the water, because polished furniture which has gone rather dull always benefits from removing the old layers of polish and giving the whole surface a fresh layer of clean polish.

On dark wood Friar's Balsam worked into the stain usually produces a good camouflage. *On very dark wood*, the colour of 'Jacobean' furniture, a mixture of olive oil and cigarette ash produces the right brown/black colour. Marks *on black lacquer* can be simply disguised with black shoe polish.

On oiled wood, such as teak, if the methylated spirit is not sufficient to bring the pale wood back to the original colour, give the mark a heavy application of teak oil before repolishing. This will be more effective if you rub the area very gently with a very fine glass paper or wire wool before applying the teak oil.

On cellulose and lacquered finishes (much modern and reproduction furniture is finished in this way) try rubbing brass polish into the mark with a soft, lint-free rag and polishing it off again before it dries. Then rub over the mark with a scorching hot duster and finish with a wax polish. If this does not work you will have to abrade the mark away with fine steel wool and restain and varnish or refinish with lacquer.

On French Polish try a proprietary French polish reviver, available from most DIY shops. In bad cases you will have to strip down the surface and repolish (see pp. 35 and 45).

Water marks (dark stains)

Because moisture causes dark stains on wood you will almost always have to get back to surface wood by abrading gently at the mark with fine grade steel wool. When you reach a fresh surface you must re-colour to match the surrounding wood. You could try the home remedies for colour matching suggested above, but having taken the trouble to reach a fresh surface it would probably be simpler to use a matching proprietary stain. When you have achieved the right shade, polish or oil the wood as necessary. Varnished wood could be treated with a tinted polyurethane stain. On dark cellulose and lacquered finishes and on French polished finishes the remedies suggested for heat marks *may* be sufficient without abrading down to fresh wood.

Ink stains

Superficial ink stains which have not penetrated the pores of the wood very deeply can be treated like water marks (see above). Where the stain has gone too deep to abrade away without making a hollow in the wood, try bleaching out the stain. First remove surface wax or polish with methylated spirit or white spirit. The professionals use sulphuric acid for bleaching as it treats most ink compounds without damaging the wood. However, because it is potentially dangerous it is not generally available and a good everyday substitute is household bleach, which should also be used with care and kept well away from children. It should be applied to the stain on a cotton wool pad to prevent it running over the entire surface. Several applications will probably be necessary to bleach out enough of the stain to make camouflage possible. Make a final application of water. Allow to dry and sand gently to get a smooth surface again. Recolour and refinish to match the original.

Alcohol

Alcohol is a solvent and will dissolve several types of wood finishes if spilled on them. It is not only found in drinks but in many cosmetic preparations and perfumes. It is essential to mop up spills immediately before the solvent starts to work. Afterwards, rub the area briskly with a little teak or linseed oil, or even with the palm of your hand if there is nothing else available. More difficult marks should be treated with one of these oils mixed to a paste with rottenstone, a mild abrasive powder. After any of these treatments re-wax the surface of the wood. Old alcohol stains will have to be abraded away and the surface of the wood refinished to match the original.

Cigarette burns

Superficial stains can be treated as water/heat marks, and will generally require you to clean back to the original wood. Unfortunately many cigarette burns go deep into the wood. If this requires you to make a hollow in the surface as you abrade away the charred wood, you will have to build it up again to make a level surface. The simplest way to do this is to use plastic wood. This is the best method if you are going to repaint the area, although even for stained wood surfaces you should be able to buy a reasonable match. It is possible to mix the standard colours to get a more exact match. You may prefer to leave a fairly shallow hollow and hope that by refinishing it to match its surroundings it will not attract the eye as the cigarette burn did.

Scratches

The simplest way to deal with scratches is to colour them with a matching stain. Several manufacturers make a 'Scratch Remover' which is just a small bottle of stain and an applicator brush which makes it easy to fill in very narrow scratches. It can be bought in light or dark shades. Children's wax crayons are also useful for disguising scratches or you could try a matching shade of shoe polish applied on a baby swab.

Dents

The sort of dent which occurs when a heavy object is dropped on a wood surface can be removed with a little care and patience. The weight has compressed the wood fibres which can be plumped out again by swelling them out with a steam treatment. First clean the wax or polish off the surface; the steam should be able to penetrate the wood without removing any of the rest of the finish. Place a damp cloth, folded to create several thicknesses, over the dent. Hold a medium hot iron on the damp cloth for a short time to create plenty of steam. Do this several times, being careful not to apply the heat for too long or after the cloth is dry, in case it harms the finish.

Using glue

Wooden furniture which has loose and wobbly joints must be dismantled and reassembled using fresh adhesive. Occasionally a clean break on something like a chair splat or leg also requires repair with adhesive. Modern adhesives generally give a reliable repair on wooden furniture, although for joints which will be taking a lot of strain it may be advisable to reinforce the repair by dowelling (see p. 13ff), with nails, screws (see p. 21) or metal plates and wooden blocks (see p. 72). The traditional woodworker's glue is Scotch glue, which is bought in crystal form and melted down in a glue pot. This has two major disadvantages: it is water soluble, and being organic it is also susceptible to fungus growths. However because the consistency is readily controllable it is still frequently used for repairing veneer (see p. 32). Epoxy adhesives are excellent for use with wood, and are totally waterproof and thus ideal for outdoor repairs. There are several quick-drying brands of epoxy adhesive available as well as the standard type. The disadvantage of epoxy adhesives is that they can cause unpleasant skin irritation and so cannot be applied in the simple, time-honoured way—with the fingers. The standard woodworking adhesives are less expensive than epoxy adhesives, but impact adhesives, which have to be left to dry for a period before pressing the two surfaces together, are not always suitable for wood. Check maker's instructions before buying for use with wood.

Method

All traces of old glue, grease and dirt should be removed from surfaces which are to be reglued (see Solvents p. 147). After cleaning, the surfaces should be allowed to dry thoroughly. Adhesive should be applied to one or both surfaces according to the maker's instructions, using your fingers or a spatula. Where it has not been possible to dismantle the join, when refixing a chair rung for example, a plastic syringe is the best tool for applying adhesive (diagram 1).

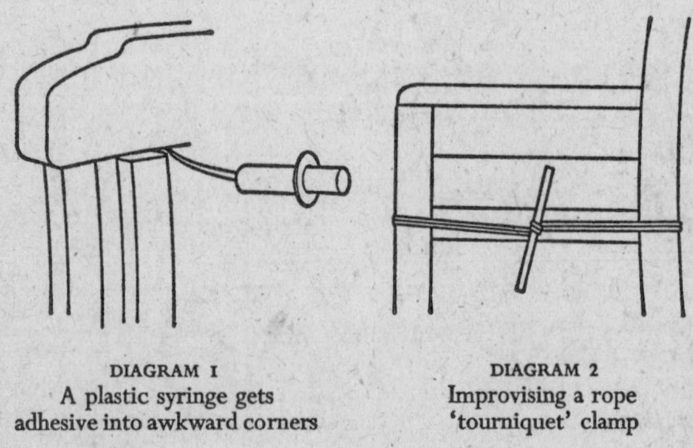

DIAGRAM 1
A plastic syringe gets adhesive into awkward corners

DIAGRAM 2
Improvising a rope 'tourniquet' clamp

Once the two sides have been brought together they must be given ample time for the adhesive to harden and during this period pressure must be applied to the joint to prevent it from slipping and to keep out as much air as possible. Suitable clamps, such as a rope tourniquet, can be improvised (diagram 2), but for best results you should use special clamps available from woodwork and DIY shops. There are different types of clamp suitable for different types of repair (diagram 3). Some of these clamps have wooden jaws which will not damage the wood when they are screwed tightly to apply the necessary pressure. If clamps do not have these wooden jaws you must remember to put something such as a block of wood or thick layers of felt between the jaws of the clamp and the furniture itself or the metal will bite into the wood of the furniture you are repairing and cause deep scars. Practise aligning the two sides and fixing the clamps to the join *before* you apply the adhesive. This is particularly important if you use epoxy or impact adhesives as the speed with which they dry

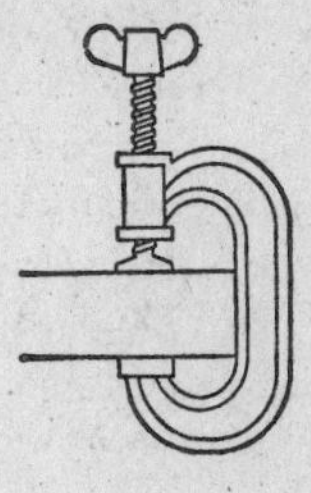

DIAGRAM 3
Two types of standard woodworkers' clamp

allows for no adjustment once contact is made. If you are unsure of your skill use a white woodworking adhesive which gives you a better chance of some last-minute adjustment.

Excess glue should be wiped away immediately if possible, unless this risks pushing the join out of alignment. Epoxy adhesives cannot be removed by solvents at a later stage. Once allowed to harden they must be abraded away.

When the adhesive has had adequate time to harden, remove the clamps and retouch the damaged wood to match the surrounding finish.

Dowelling

Using a dowel (wooden peg)
Dowelling in conjunction with glueing is the best way to mend a chair leg which has snapped fairly cleanly into two. It is usually the front leg which breaks in this way when it is tipped forward. You may also wish to replace original dowelling which has broken. Old dowelling should always be thoroughly cleaned out, by drilling it out if necessary. Any traces of old glue should be removed with a solvent. Properly grooved dowelling can be bought from DIY shops in varying diameters or you can make your own dowels out of spare bits of wood. Home-made dowels or smooth lengths of dowelling must be

grooved to allow air and excess glue to escape back up the dowelling hole. Do this by gripping the dowel with serrated pliers and pulling them along the length of the wood (diagram 1).

DIAGRAM 1
Groove dowelling peg with serrated pliers

Method

The principles of joining two pieces of wood by dowelling are shown in diagram 6 which illustrates the complete repair. Holes are drilled in the centre of the two pieces to be joined to a depth of 5 cm on either side. This would require a piece of dowelling fractionally shorter than 10 cm. If longer dowels are needed to give the required strength you can buy extra long bits for the drill. Drill the holes with a bit which has a diameter slightly larger than the dowel. The hole should be narrow enough to hold the dowel snugly without requiring you to hammer it home and risk splitting the surrounding wood. To get a really good fit use a dowel bit, which is more accurately sized than an ordinary auger bit.

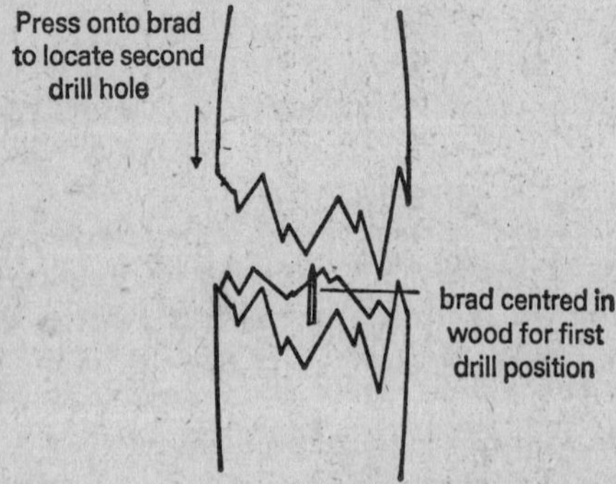

DIAGRAM 2
Use a brad to locate drill

The problem at this stage is to centre the holes accurately on both sides. If you are going to do a lot of furniture-making or repair you can invest in a dowelling jig. Otherwise a simple way of centring a dowel is to hammer a narrow brad (a nail without a head) right into the centre of the end of one of the broken pieces, (diagram 2). It is not difficult to do this, especially if you take the additional precaution of measuring up the centre and marking it, rather than making an inspired guess. Fit the two pieces together as accurately as possible and press them together so that the end of the brad marks the raw edge of the opposite half of the break. Pull the brad out with a pair of pliers and use the marks it has made on both sides as the guide for the drilling (diagram 3).

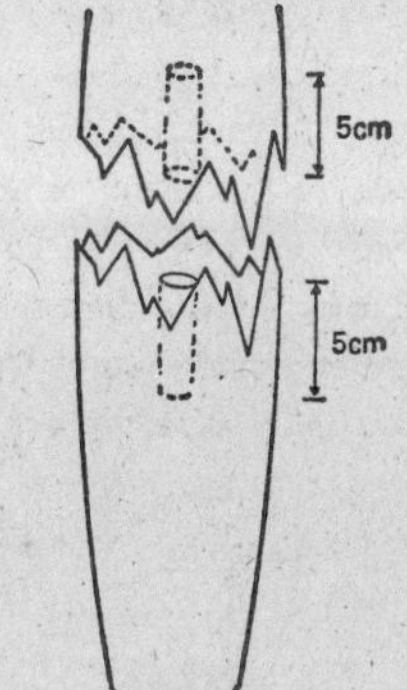

DIAGRAM 3
Drill holes to receive dowel

The dowelling repair is strengthened by glue. Apply a thin layer to one half of the dowel. Fit the dowel into one of the holes. (This will be simpler if you taper the ends of the dowel first). Any excess glue which is forced out can be spread over the raw edge of the broken wood and extra added if necessary (diagram 4). Next apply glue to the second half of the dowel and fit the second piece of broken wood over it (diagram 5). The raw edge of this should also have a thin application of glue. Press the two halves firmly together and wipe off any excess glue which oozes out. The join should be securely clamped together until the glue has dried. Afterwards you can finish off the job by camouflaging any marks with a little stain or polish which blends in with the surrounding wood.

DIAGRAM 4
Fitting dowel into hole

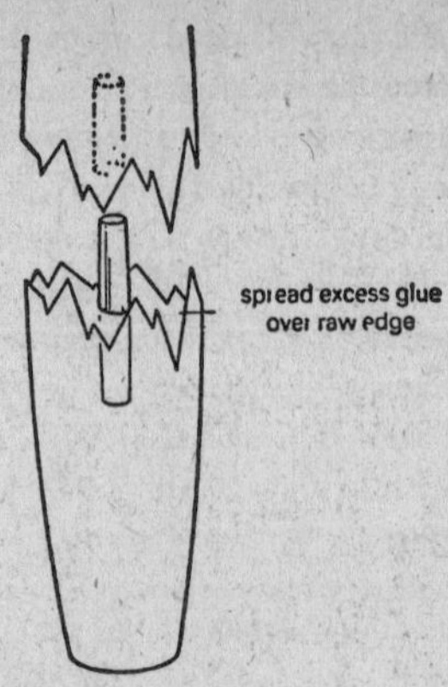

DIAGRAM 5
Fitting the two halves together

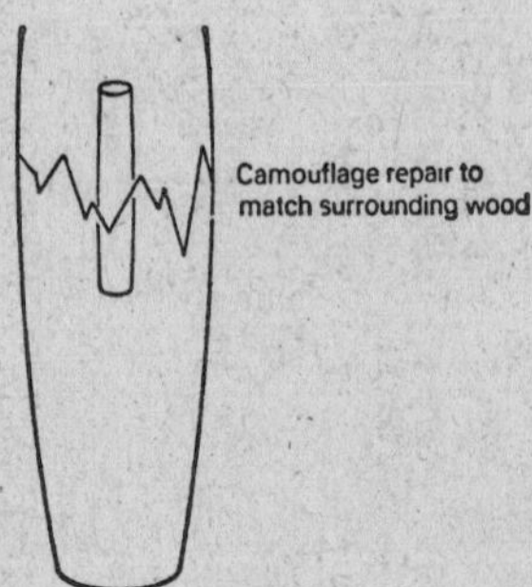

DIAGRAM 6
Dowelling repair completed

Making a mortise and tenon joint (Advanced) (diagrams 1–5)

You cannot replace a mortise and tenon joint (see below) without knowing how to make a new one. Since this requires a certain amount of skill and practice you may not consider it worthwhile for simply mending a joint. If you would like to repair a mortise and tenon joint yourself you will need a mortise gauge, a mortise chisel (preferably to match the width of the tenon you intend to make), a mallet and a woodworker's vice for holding the wood securely while you make the joint. If you do not expect to be making many of the same type of joint but think you will be doing quite a bit of repair work involving several different types of joints, you may prefer to invest in a piece of equipment called a Jointmaster. This enables you to measure and cut several different types of joint accurately and comes with instructions for making them all. Although it is quite expensive it is not as expensive as buying equipment such as a mortise gauge and using it only once.

To make a mortise and tenon joint, measure the width and position of the mortise with the mortise gauge (diagram 4). Chip out the

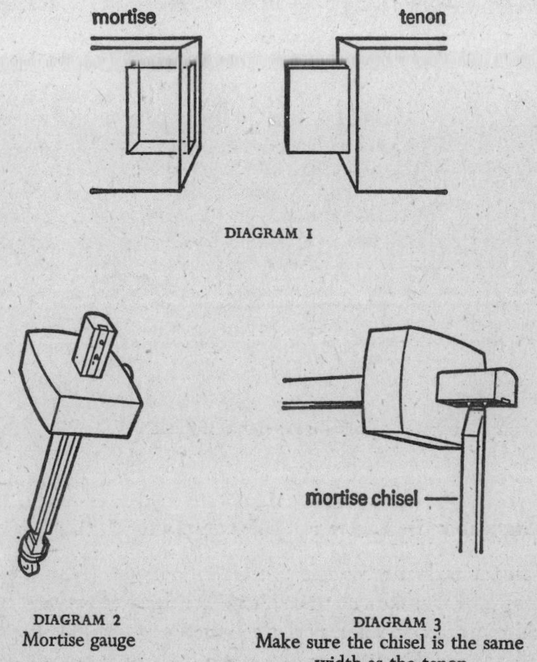

DIAGRAM 1

DIAGRAM 2
Mortise gauge

DIAGRAM 3
Make sure the chisel is the same width as the tenon

mortise with a wide mortise chisel and a mallet (diagram 5). When the mortise is cut measure out the tenon to fit it, using the mortise gauge again. Holding the wood in a vice, saw out the tenon, making it a fraction larger to allow for fine adjustments. Sand down if necessary to make a perfect fit with the mortise, then glue and clamp the two components of the joint as usual.

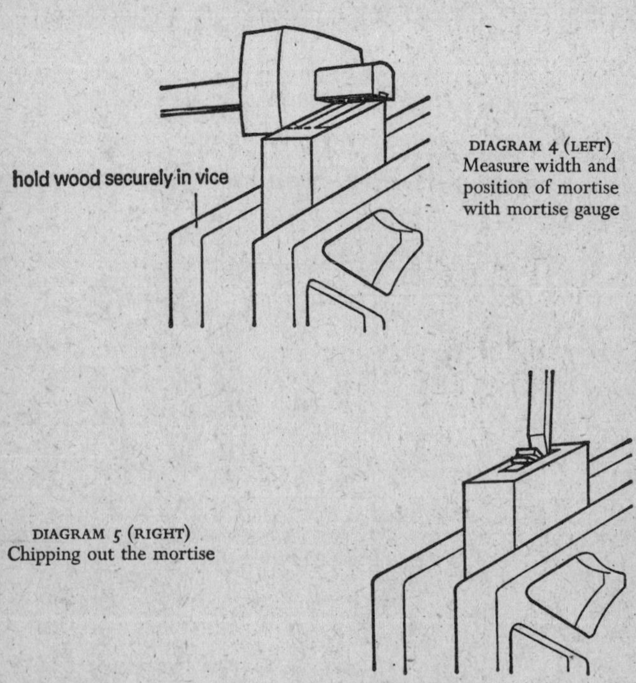

DIAGRAM 4 (LEFT)
Measure width and position of mortise with mortise gauge

DIAGRAM 5 (RIGHT)
Chipping out the mortise

Repairs

Insecure mortise and tenon joints, like most other types, can usually be strengthened with metal plates or wood blocks (see p. 72). Alternatively they may simply need to be taken apart, cleaned and reglued. This is preferable if there is any chance of the repair being seen. Occasionally the wood of the joint is damaged and will need to be repaired. Either the tenon is broken (diagram 6), or the wood of the mortise has splintered.

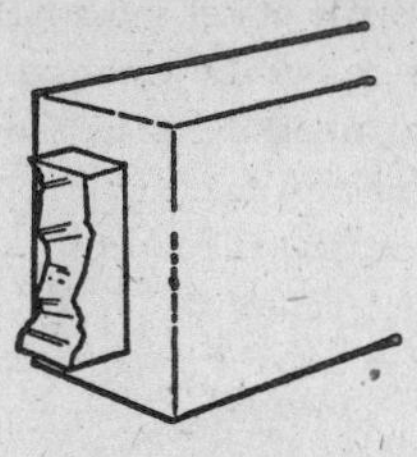

DIAGRAM 6
Damaged tenon

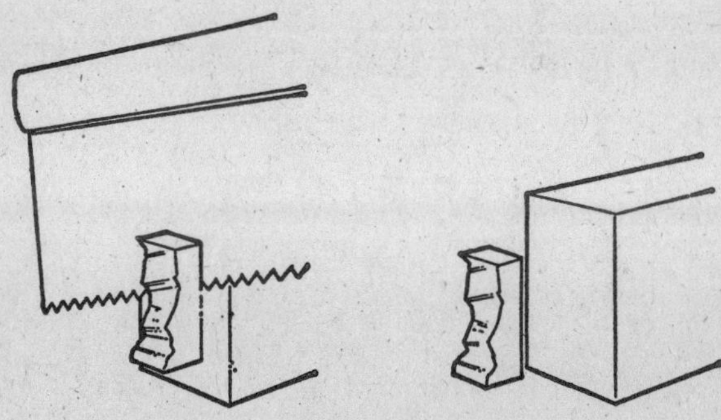

DIAGRAM 7a and b
Cut away damaged tenon to leave flat surface of undamaged wood

Mending a broken tenon (diagrams 7–9)
Take the joint apart and cut away the damaged tenon flush with the surrounding wood (diagram 7). Cut a new mortise into *this* side of the join to match the existing mortise. Now cut a fresh tenon *twice* the length of the original (diagram 8). Glue this into the new mortise. Allow sufficient time for the glue to dry thoroughly. If the joint is to take a lot of strain you may feel it necessary to run a dowelling peg through the whole thing to strengthen it further (diagram 9 and p. 13). When the new tenon is firmly in position, slot it into the original mortise, glueing and applying pressure to the join in the usual way.

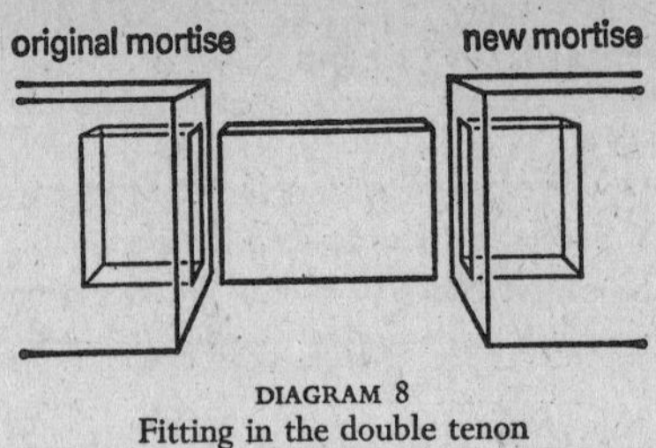

DIAGRAM 8
Fitting in the double tenon

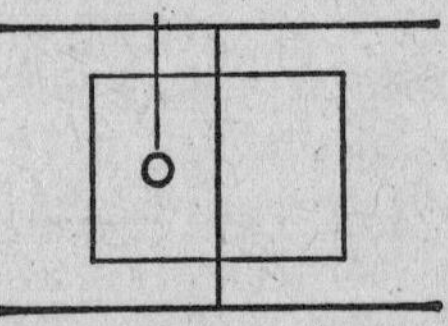

DIAGRAM 9
Strengthening repair with dowelling peg

Replacing a damaged mortise (diagrams 10 and 11)
Where the mortise wood is damaged, cut right back to sound wood (diagram 10). Glue on a fresh block of wood to replace what you have removed (diagram 11). (Blockboard would be a good substitute.) Use a good quality wood glue, apply sufficient pressure to the repair and allow to dry thoroughly. You can then cut a new mortise into this fresh wood.

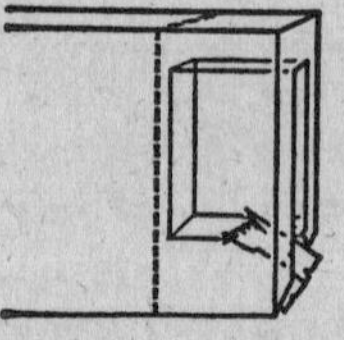

DIAGRAM 10
Cut off damaged wood

DIAGRAM 11
Replace damaged section and cut new mortise

Removing and replacing screws

Removing old screws

The obvious way of removing screws is simply to unscrew them with a screwdriver. However it is rarely a simple job in old furniture, especially if the screw has rusted into the wood or the thread has broken. If you are having trouble removing screws, first clean the head of old paint and varnish, and then brush a little paraffin or clock oil around the head. Give this lubrication plenty of time to soak in round the screw and then try again with the screwdriver. If you have a brace with a screwdriving bit, you will get more pressure to bear on the screw, but take care that you do not overdo the pressure so that the screwdriver jumps out of the narrow slot in the screw head and scratches the surrounding wood.

If the screw remains obstinately in place there are two more drastic measures you can take. The first is to apply a heated metal rod to the head of the screw. This will cause the metal to expand. With luck this will also enlarge the screw hole in the wood, enabling the screw to be removed easily when the metal cools down again. If this does not work, scrape away dirt and a little of the wood from underneath the head of the screw so that it stands out enough for you to grip the head with pliers and pull it out. The damage done to the wood will have to be made good by refinishing and by building up the missing wood with plastic wood if necessary.

Putting in new screws (see also *Replacing handles, hinges and locks on wood*)

You can avoid the problem of rusted-in screws in the future if you use brass screws. A little wax on the shank will also reduce rusting and will make it easier to drive the screw into the wood.

When using screws in hardwood you will need to drill two holes of different sizes and ideally a countersink hole as well to accommodate the head of the screw so that it lies flush with the surface of the wood, (diagram 1). This can be camouflaged with plastic wood, coloured wax or paint to match the surrounding wood (see p. 47). The length of the screw will vary and it is best to drill the thread hole a little short to avoid the problem of an oversize hole. The table

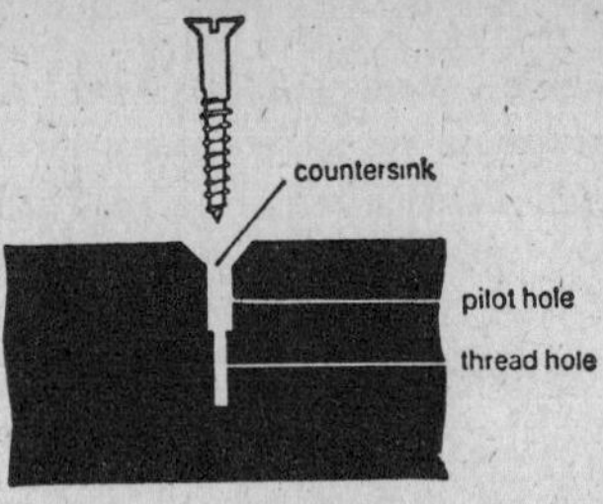

DIAGRAM I

below shows the standard drill sizes for the pilot hole and thread hole in hard wood.

For softwoods drill a pilot hole the same size as for hardwoods. There will probably be no need to drill a thread hole. If you do have difficulty in getting a screw into softwood, drill a thread hole, but one that is smaller than the standard size for hardwoods.

If you are re-using old screws you can match them against new ones to find their diameter and the hole sizes you need to drill.

Gauge of screw	*Pilot hole* mm	*(in)*	*Thread hole* mm	*(in)*
4	3	(1/8)	2	(5/64)
6	4	(5/32)	2	(5/64)
8	5	(3/16)	2.5	(3/32)
10	5.5	(7/32)	3	(1/8)
12	6	(1/4)	3	(1/8)

Replacing handles, hinges and locks, strengthening base wood

Handles, hinges and locks on wooden furniture may fall out or be too loose to be effective because the wood to which they are attached has become damaged. This type of damage can frequently be avoided if the furniture is treated properly. For example, do not push doors back further than they can comfortably go as this puts too much strain on the hinges. The flaps of drop-fronted desks should never be allowed to fall without any support or be used without the pull-out supports.

Wooden handles

Wooden handles have a stem which is glued into the drawer itself (diagram 1). When these are loose remove them, clean off the old glue by abrading and solvents (see p. 147) and refix them using fresh adhesive. If the hole into which the stem fits seems too large, wrap a layer of plywood veneer, which can be bought in strips, round the stem so that it fits firmly. Additional strength can be given to a wooden handle which takes a lot of strain by adding a section of wood to the inside of the drawer and running a screw through it into the stem of the handle (diagram 2).

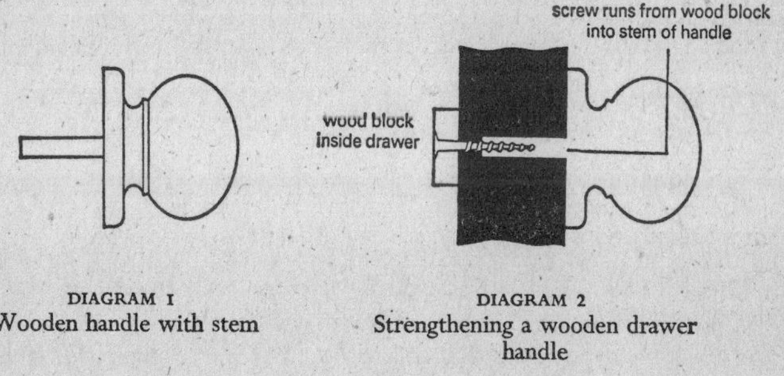

DIAGRAM 1
Wooden handle with stem

DIAGRAM 2
Strengthening a wooden drawer handle

Metal handles, hinges and locks

Where handles, hinges or locks are loose because the screw holes are enlarged, but surrounding wood remains undamaged, plug the enlarged hole with plastic wood or dowelling pegs trimmed to size (very small holes can be plugged with a mixture of adhesive and thin slivers of wood packed into the hole). When these repairs are dry you will have a secure base into which you can rescrew the handle, hinge or lock (see p. 21, for removing old screws and fixing new screws).

Where the wood around handles, hinges or locks is clearly splintered and damaged it will be necessary to remove the entire section and replace it to improve its strength and appearance (diagram 3). When the metal fitting is removed, cut around the damaged wood to reach sound wood. After the damaged wood is removed, you

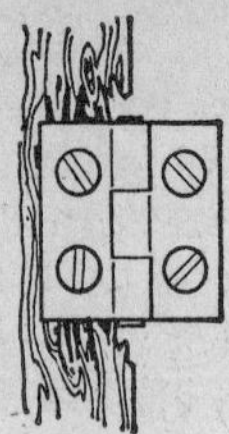

DIAGRAM 3
Hinge is loose because surrounding wood is damaged

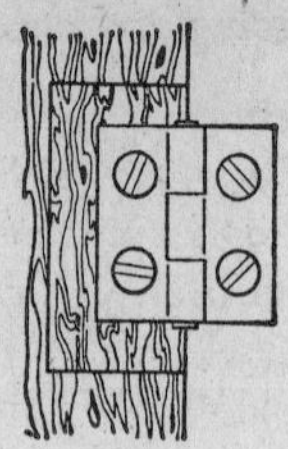

DIAGRAM 4
Damaged base wood replaced and hinge screwed into it

should make sure that you have a regular-shaped gap to fill. Glue a fresh block of wood into the gap to replace the damaged wood you have removed. Finish this new wood to match the surrounding wood as closely as possible. Since the area is usually very small, a little coloured polyurethane stain will probably do an adequate job. Now the handle, hinge or lock can be screwed back into place using fresh screws (diagram 4). If you are replacing a lock you may need to recut the mortise slot into fresh wood, replacing as described on p. 20. Do this with a mortise chisel and mallet. The deep mortise for sinking a metal plate should be cut into the wood last of all (see diagrams 5 and 6, and also p. 78).

DIAGRAM 5
Replace damaged base wood of metal mortise with new wood cut to a regular shape

DIAGRAM 6
Cut mortise into fresh wood and replace metal plate

Replacing and mending broken castors

The castors on old furniture are often broken but even more often it is the wood to which they are fixed which is damaged. You are unlikely to be able to buy a replacement to match the rest of the castors on your piece of furniture, since modern castors come in a very limited selection. If you think you will be mending a lot of furniture, it would therefore be a good idea to keep any old castors in good condition on pieces of furniture which you throw away. If you replace *one* castor you should replace them all, unless you find a replacement which lifts the leg to exactly the same height off the ground.

There are 4 basic types of castor:

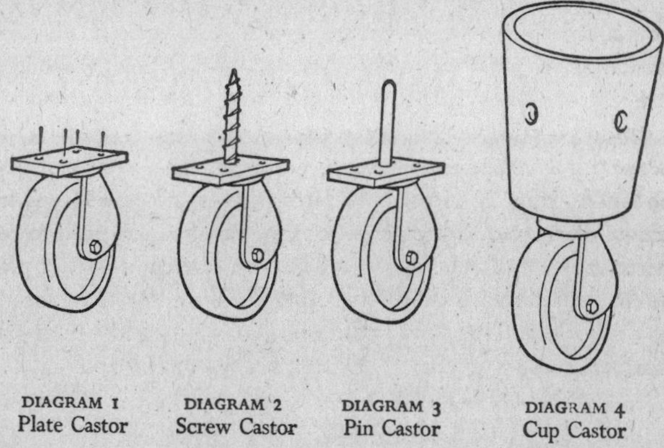

DIAGRAM 1 Plate Castor

DIAGRAM 2 Screw Castor

DIAGRAM 3 Pin Castor

DIAGRAM 4 Cup Castor

1. (diagram 1) *Plate Castor* Attached to the leg by a flat plate screwed into the wood with short screws. This is the weakest type and only suitable for light duty. Do not replace any of the others with this type.
2. (diagram 2) *Screw Castor* Looks like 1. but has a long central screw as well as the short screws for attaching the plate. This is the commonest type.
3. (diagram 3) *Pin Castor* As 2. but has a central pin, not a central screw.
4. (diagram 4) *Cup Castor* Has a cup which fits round the end of the leg and is screwed in at the sides.

When doing any of the following repairs clean the castor and remove rust, then oil with a light general-purpose oil before replacing.

The commonest failure with 1. is that the screws have worked loose. Remove the castor and refix, moving the plate round so that the screws go into fresh wood. *N.B.* if the wood is badly damaged you may need to saw off a thin layer to get to fresh wood; remember to remove an equal thickness of wood on all the legs or the furniture will not stand properly. This note also applies to types 2, and 3.

The commonest failure with 2. is that the central screw has worked loose. If the screw hole has simply become a little enlarged you could replace the original castor with one which has a wider screw which will still get a grip in the wood. Pin castors usually have a pin which is thicker than a screw and using one of these may be sufficient to fill the excess space. A cup castor will avoid the problem altogether. Be sure to find a replacement which has the same lift off the ground. When replacing, position the plate so that the small screws bite into fresh wood (see note for type 1). If you cannot find a suitable replacement, or if the wood has become damaged around the screw hole, this hole should be plugged with fresh wood. Do this by running a little woodworking adhesive into the hole and packing it with slivers of fresh wood. When the glue is completely hard, cut off any projecting slivers of wood flush with the end of the leg. Drill a fresh hole for the screw into this strengthened base (see p. 21 for fixing screws), and adjust the position of the base plate so that its screws also go into fresh wood.

An additional problem with screw castors is that the central screw may snap off and get stuck inside the leg. The simplest method of dealing with this is to replace the original castor with a cup castor, even though it may mean replacing all the castors in order to get the furniture to stand evenly.

Where the end of the leg is so badly damaged that there is not even a grip for the horizontal screws of a cup castor, and where cutting off the damaged section would shorten the leg too much, you may need to replace the damaged wood (diagrams 5–7). The diagrams show the principle on which this is done, but you need some aptitude for woodwork in order to do a good job. Trim off the leg above the damaged wood. Drill a hole up into the leg to take a dowelling peg. Cut a fresh piece of wood to replace the damaged section. Ideally

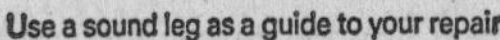

DIAGRAM 5
Trim off damaged wood

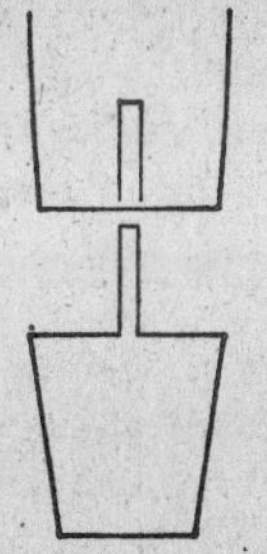

DIAGRAM 6
Skilled woodworkers can incorporate a fixing peg in the new wood

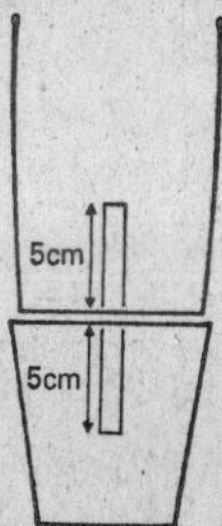

DIAGRAM 7
Use a dowel to attach fresh wood

this should also incorporate a central peg of exactly the right size and position to fit into the dowelling hole in the leg. However, trimming this integral peg is a very skilled job, and you may find it easier to use a length of standard dowelling and drill a separate central hole into the replacement wood as well as the leg itself. The dowelling pin is then glued into both sockets (see p. 15) in the usual way. To help with the problem of getting the replacement wood in exactly the right position, cut it a little larger all over than the final size. Any minor mistakes in positioning, which are almost inevitable when trying to align the dowel, can be compensated for when you trim the wood down to the right shape and size.

When the new wood is firmly fixed to the original leg, the castor can be attached in the usual way.

Repairing and replacing wooden beading and moulding

Minor damage on decorative wooden beading and moulding can be repaired by filling with plastic wood or epoxy putty. This is abraded down when dry and recoloured to match the original. Where large sections are missing it may be possible to buy replacement strips at a woodwork supply shop, some of the simpler designs having remained unchanged for years. It is a good idea to keep a box of beading and moulding taken from discarded furniture if you want to get an exact match with repairs. Where a large proportion of beading has been lost, the simplest technique may be to remove the original totally and replace it all with new beading finished to match the original. New strips of beading should be secured with adhesive and if additional security is required panel pins can be used (diagram 1).

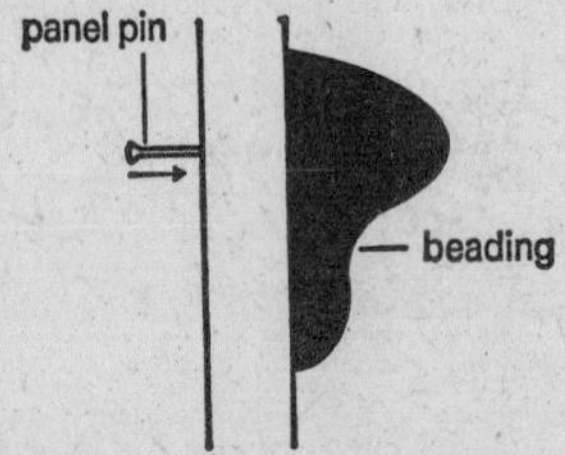

DIAGRAM 1
Attach new beading with adhesive and panel pins

Making replacement moulding (advanced)
Where moulding forms a substantial part of the furniture, on the edge of a desk for example, it may be worth taking time to shape a new piece to match, which can then be fitted into the gap in the original moulding. Cut away damaged wood so that you have a regular shape to fill (diagrams 2 and 3). Cut a section of wood to fill the width of the gap exactly, but with the other dimensions cut the wood a little larger than the overall size of the section it is to replace (diagram 4).

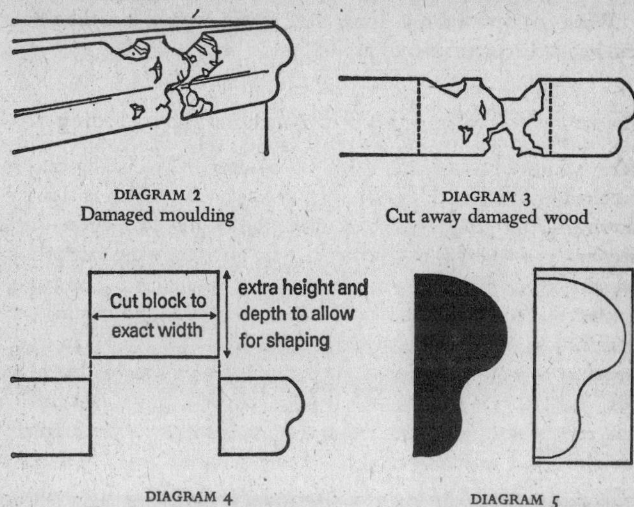

DIAGRAM 2
Damaged moulding

DIAGRAM 3
Cut away damaged wood

DIAGRAM 4
Glue in replacement wood

DIAGRAM 5
Shape block to match original moulding

This will allow for shaping. Mark the profile of the moulding on the end of the replacement section and shape it with a small carving chisel and sand paper (diagram 5). Stain to match the original wood and when dry use adhesive to fix it into the gap.

Freeing jammed and sticking drawers

If drawers are really firmly jammed you should not use force on them as you will damage the furniture. You must remove the back of the furniture and push from the back, preferably with someone to help you manipulate the drawer from the front. You will not need to do this with drawers which are merely sticking, but otherwise the remedies for both problems are usually the same, differences being simply a matter of degree. If the drawer is one of several, in a chest of drawers for instance, take out one of the sound drawers as a guide to what the damaged drawer should be like. Before doing anything more drastic, try waxing the runners of the drawer and the drawer rails.

Damp is the most common cause of sticking drawers. The moisture causes the wood to swell and go out of true. Rub chalk over the drawer and the drawer rails; the chalk will slide over the damp, indicating areas where the wood has swollen. Sand or plane away the excess wood until the drawer fits properly again. Prevent a recurrence of the trouble by sealing the wood against moisture with a polyurethane lacquer.

Drawers are often made of cheap, flimsy wood even if the front presents a good appearance. One result of this is that one of the back corners lifts up and the drawer is no longer perfectly square (diagram 1). To compensate for this you will have to sand or plane off the top edge, which will be jamming. The underside of the drawer can then be built up with slivers of wood and a good woodworking glue so that the drawer fits properly into the drawer rails again (diagram 2). Apply a little wax to help the drawer run smoothly.

Another reason for jamming is that the drawer gets rammed in

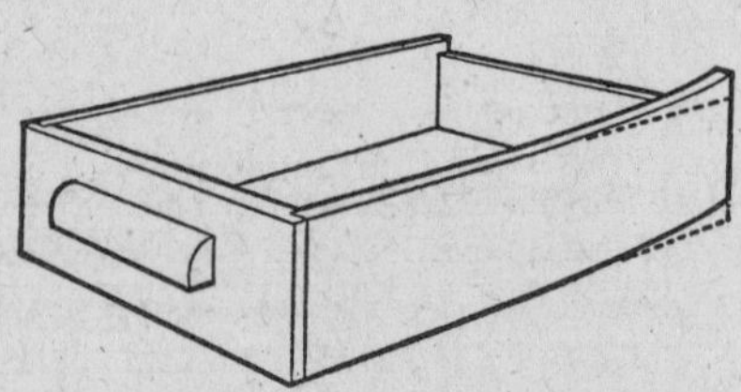

DIAGRAM 1
Poor quality wood may lift up at corners

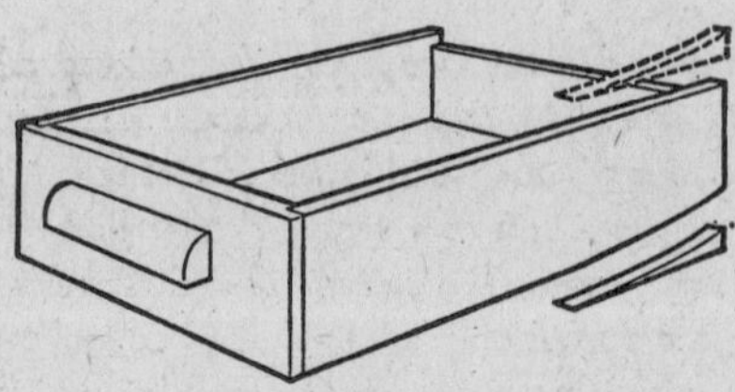

DIAGRAM 2
Restore shape by sanding off top edge and building up lower edge

too hard and the stop at the back breaks. The broken stop will have to be removed and a new one fitted. Cut a piece of wood the same size as the broken stop and fix the new stop with glue and panel pins.

Where the drawer is coming apart the best approach is to dismantle it totally, clean the joints, using a solvent to remove all traces of glue and stick it back together again (see p. 11). Use a try square to check that the corners are exactly at right angles (diagram 3).

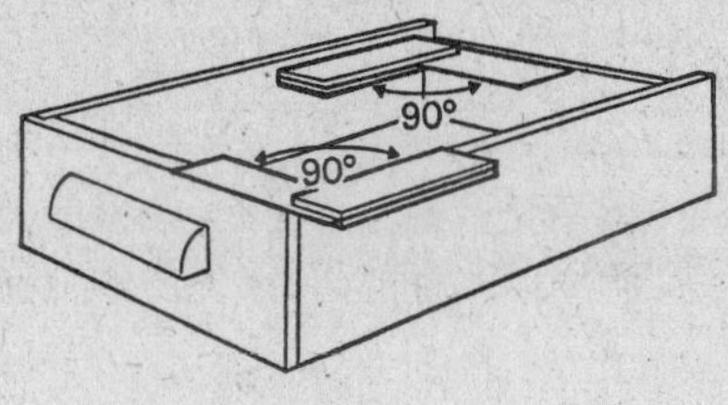

DIAGRAM 3
A try square ensures accurate corners

Repairing damaged veneer (Advanced)

There are two basic repairs to veneer. The first is replacement of a section which has been chipped off completely; the second is regluing veneer which has lifted away from the base wood. In both cases if the damage is not very obvious it is probably better left alone, particularly if you are not able to get a good match for a piece of veneer which has been lost.

Replacing missing veneer

If you do a lot of restoration work you should keep odd scraps of veneer from furniture which is past repair as this will give you a stock from which you may be able to find a suitable match. A professional cabinet maker may have left-over scraps of the good quality woods such as walnut and rosewood which are used for veneer work. It is important to match up not only the type of wood and the shade but also the grain, as this forms an integral part of the overall pattern. You may be able to plane a suitably wafer-thin sliver off a block of the correct type of wood.

Cut out the damaged section (diagram 1) with a sharp single-edged razor blade, a Stanley knife or a scalpel. Try to make a simple shape such as a square or a diamond which will be easy to copy. Avoid cutting across the grain of the veneer if at all possible, as this may cause the cut to have ragged edges.

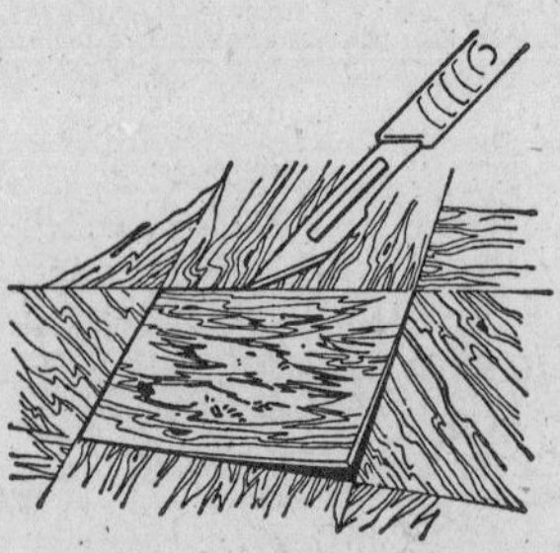

DIAGRAM 1
Remove damaged wood

Trace the outline of the section to be replaced (diagram 2) and stick the tracing of the outline down on the back of the veneer which you are using for the replacement. Secure it in position and go over the original line with a pencil, outlining the shape. The grain should follow the same line as the original (diagram 3). Cut out the replacement patch. Cut a little larger than the pattern if you are unsure of your skill, as it is simpler to sand off excess from the edges than to

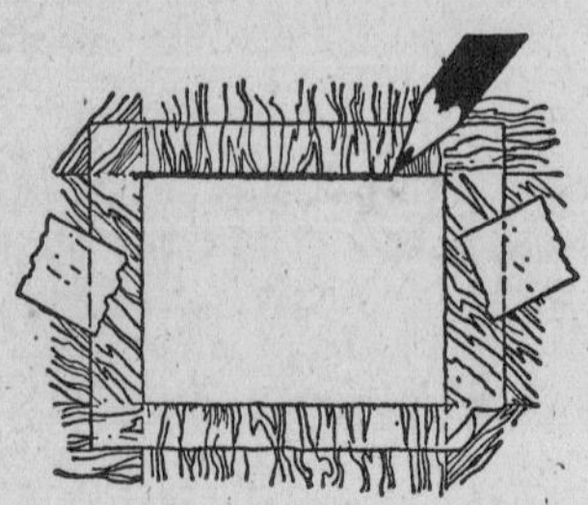

DIAGRAM 2
Trace the shape to be replaced

DIAGRAM 3
Replacement patch should have same grain as original

start all over again. Scrape away all excess glue from the base wood and wipe with a cotton-wool swab of methylated spirit to make sure that the area is free of grease. Stick the patch into position with a modern woodworker's adhesive, sparingly applied. Wipe away excess glue immediately and weight the repair until the glue has dried thoroughly. When the patch is firmly in position, polish the whole area so that it blends in.

An alternative adhesive is Scotch glue which was always used for veneering because it is water-soluble. This makes it easy to remove a piece of veneer which has already been stuck down. Use warmed Scotch glue reconstituted according to manufacturer's instructions if you anticipate making several attemps at replacing the missing veneer. Remove veneer stuck down with Scotch glue by steaming it off, using a warm iron over a damp cloth.

Resticking lifted veneer

Veneer which has lifted a little from the base wood because it has been kept in over-dry conditions can be stuck down again. Lift the veneer as high as it will go, taking care not to push it too far and snap it off. Scrape away as much of the old glue as possible using a small, sharp knife (diagram 4). Where the original veneer has been stuck down with the traditional Scotch glue, you may be able to wipe away some of the glue with a little warm water. When the wood is

DIAGRAM 4
Old glue must be removed

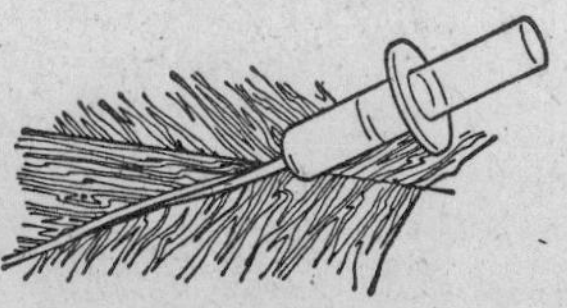

DIAGRAM 5
A syringe gets adhesive under loose veneer

clean and dry apply a thin smear of adhesive to the base wood and underside of the veneer. Use a palette knife or even a syringe if the opening is very small (diagram 5). Press the veneer down and wipe away any excess glue. Weight or clamp the repair until the adhesive dries. A pad of felt or piece of wood placed between the clamp and the veneer will prevent damage to the surface of the veneer (diagram 6).

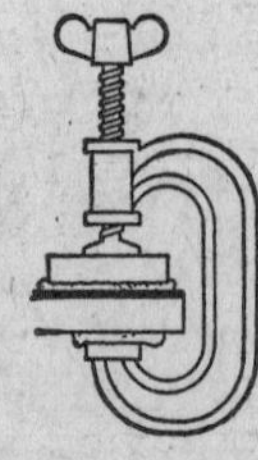

DIAGRAM 6
Protect surface when using clamps

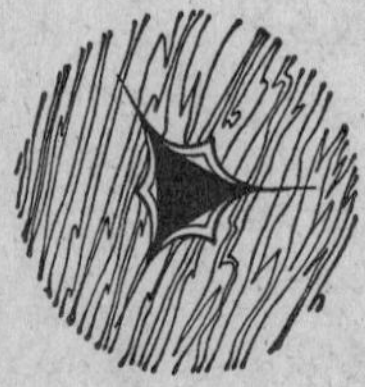

DIAGRAM 7
Cut into a raised 'bubble' of veneer and reglue it

If the centre of the veneer has lifted up in a bubble, you can repair it in exactly the same way as veneer which has lifted from the edge. In order to get under the bubble to clean away the old, dried-out glue and apply fresh adhesive, make a three-way cut in the centre with a sharp single-edged razor blade (diagram 7).

4
Refinishing

Cleaning and removing old finishes from wood

You can remove an old finish by heat, by sanding or by a chemical solvent. The heat method, with a blow lamp or similar tool, is generally impractical. It can be dangerous and the effects of the heat are usually too powerful for all but the roughest furniture. The best way to remove old finishes is usually to begin with a chemical solvent and use sanding for the finishing touches so that you get a good smooth surface to take the new finish.

Cleaning the wood

Before going to the trouble of stripping off an old finish completely, clean the furniture thoroughly. You may find that cleaning and/or rewaxing will be all you need to get it looking good again. Even if you are not so lucky, cleaning will make it easier to determine the state of your furniture. In some cases you may decide that it is not sturdy enough to stand up to the onslaught of full-scale stripping and refinishing. In such a case it would be better to use refinishing methods to retouch damaged areas, matching the original as closely as possible (see different techniques for refinishing wood p. 41 on). Minor damage can usually be camouflaged without stripping down to bare wood (see Simple repairs for burns, scratches etc. on wood p. 8).

Cleaning can be a quite simple matter of washing the wood with a detergent solution applied with a sponge or chamois leather. Be sure to rinse off all traces of the detergent solution with several applications of clean water. Do not slop water all over the piece of furniture and make sure the sponge or wash-leather is well rung out. Too much water can loosen glued joints or raise the grain of the wood. Make sure the wood has had time to dry thoroughly before starting on minor repairs or complete stripping. After waxed wood has been washed (or before if the wood is not grubby), dull wax polish can be removed with methylated spirit or white spirit (turpentine substitute) and the furniture brought back to condition with a fresh application of a good quality white wax polish.

Stripping with chemicals

Paint removers are suitable for most varnishes as well as paint. Try to choose one specified as not inflammable and which can be washed off and removed from delicate surfaces without risking damage from a metal paint scraper. Incidentally remember when washing paint remover away that too much water may raise the grain of the wood and loosen glued joints.

Paint remover should be applied liberally with a large paint brush. Ideally this should be done outside but if you have to work indoors minimise any danger from fumes by working in a well-ventilated room as near an open window as possible. Protect your clothing and hands. Make sure the floor is covered with something more substantial than newspaper, which will quickly soak up any spills. Work over one surface at a time so that vertical surfaces can be turned to horizontal while they are being worked on. If you have to work on a vertical surface place a container underneath to catch the inevitable drips.

After 10 minutes or so, when the paint remover starts to bubble up, it should be possible to start removing the old finish. Do not let the paint remover dry before starting to take off the finish. If it starts to dry before you have finished, add more paint remover. Wipe or wash off the old finish using a soft scrubbing brush to loosen it. Use a metal paint scraper only if really necessary, as these almost inevitably gouge into the wood. New metal paint scrapers should have the sharp edges blunted by a file if they are to be used on furniture. You may find the edge of a piece of wood does the job of scraping just as well, without the risk of denting the wood. Where washing does not work sufficiently well or cannot be used at all, for instance on a veneer which would be lifted up by water, and yet the surface is too delicate for a scraper of any kind, use the paint stripper in conjunction with a pad of fine (grade 000) steel wool. This is much more time-consuming but far gentler.

Carved wood should be stripped in a horizontal position so that the paint remover does not run out of the nooks and crannies. A soft brush, such as a used toothbrush, can be used to remove residue. If this is not strong enough scrape gently with a wooden spatula or orange stick.

When this stage is completed wash down the surface or apply a neutraliser if the manufacturer's instructions specify one. Take care to get into all the crevices of carved and turned furniture. The wood should then be allowed a few days to dry out completely.

Sanding

You can strip off an old finish completely by sanding. Doing this by hand involves a lot of hard work and the obvious answer for removing the bulk of the old finish is to use a power sander. Unfortunately most of these have a circular movement which cuts across the grain of the wood, and one of the basic rules of sanding is to go with the grain of the wood so as to avoid making scratches which will be emphasised rather than disguised when the new finish is applied. If you do have a disc attachment for an all-purpose power tool it would be better to use it at a later stage with a polishing pad for bringing up a shine. For all but the largest and roughest furniture remove as much as possible of the finish with a chemical paint remover and then sand by hand to prepare the wood for the new finish. For very bulky objects you might consider it worthwhile to hire a sander which has a straight line action which can be used along the grain of the wood.

After using paint stripper and allowing the wood time to dry, take a look at your furniture and do any necessary repairs including treating for woodworm before sanding so that the article will be totally ready for the new finish when you have completed this stage. This means that you will only have to sand once. If you do repairs at a later stage you will find yourself going over the same area again to remove dried glue, roughened wood or the excess of fillers such as plastic wood which have been used to fill dents and scratches.

For work on furniture use a really good quality glass paper. This will be cheaper in the long run because a good quality paper will not only be faster to work with but will also give a better finish. If possible ask for an open coat paper which does not clog up as quickly as the more densely covered type. If you are sanding only to give the surface a final preparation for the new finish then fine grade or flour grade will be all you need. This is intended for delicate work and will not scratch the surface. For rougher work choose a coarse grade and finish off with the finer grade.

Sand with the grain of the wood, never across the grain (diagram 1). Wrap the abrasive paper round a sanding block. This is a wooden block with a felt-covered base which helps to keep scratching to a minimum and has grooves along the sides to give a firm grip. The sanding block evens out the pressure you apply to the wood and avoids a common beginner's mistake—rubbing grooves into the wood with sandpaper wrapped round one finger. Take care not to take the block constantly over the edges of a flat surface or you will round them off. Of course, if you want rounded edges this is the way to do it.

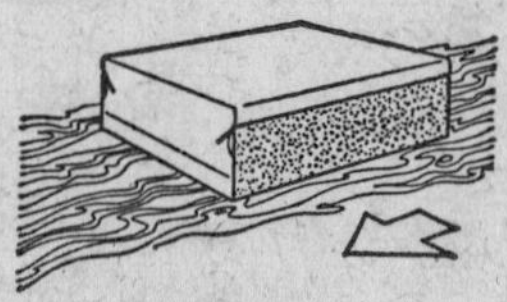

DIAGRAM 1
Use a sanding block for even pressure and work along the grain of the wood

A standard flat sanding block will be no help for curved surfaces like chair backs. For these you will have to improvise by wrapping the sandpaper around a length of round wood, a broom handle for example. For chair legs *etc.* fold a strip of sandpaper, giving it extra strength by backing it with stiff card if necessary, and use it like a belt or bathtowel (diagrams 2 and 3). Fine (grade 000) steel wool can be used on carved surfaces.

Take great care to ensure even pressure, as a surface which has not been given uniform treatment will not take a finish evenly. It is up to you how much trouble you wish to take with the preparation of the wood before refinishing. The better quality the wood, the more worthwhile the extra effort. A softwood such as pine (deal) will not

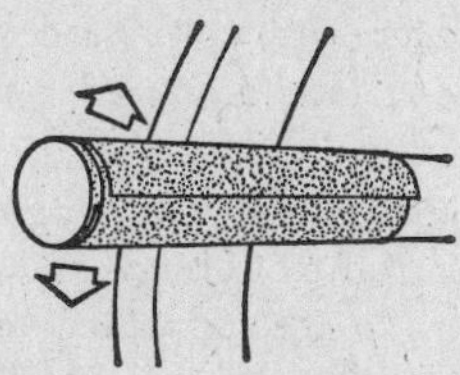

DIAGRAM 2
Wrap abrasive paper round a round handle to sand curved surfaces

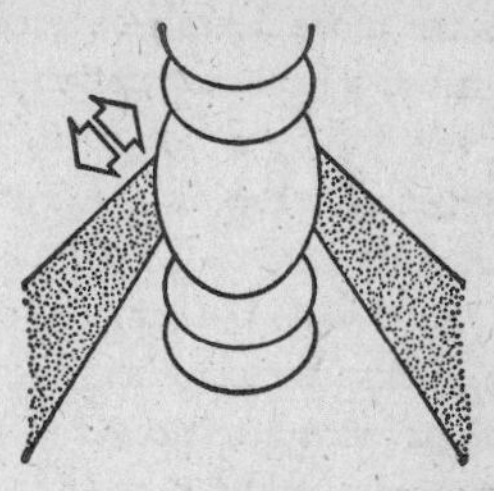

DIAGRAM 3
Use sandpaper like a bathtowel on rounded surfaces

benefit much from work with a really fine sandpaper, but a good quality hardwood will repay a little extra trouble.

If you are going to paint the wood it is not worth doing more than making sure that the surface has no scratches or blemishes which will show up through the paint. On the other hand if you intend to use a 'natural' stained and varnished finish, the final effect will only be as good as the preparation you have put into the wood.

Bleaching

If, even after sanding, your wood has patches of discolouration remaining from the previous finish, and if the paint stripper has darkened or dulled the wood, or you prefer a lighter colour, you can bleach the wood at this stage. With any luck ordinary domestic bleach will be sufficiently strong for your purposes; after all, wood is naturally variegated in colour and a uniform result is not desirable. Alternatively some manufacturers market a bleach specifically for wood. However, if the problem remains after you have used domestic bleach or wood bleach you can then try the more traditional remedies: hydrogen peroxide (20 volume or stronger), sodium hypochlorite, or oxalic acid. Try to avoid using these if at all possible; indeed you may have great difficulty getting hold of the last two unless you know someone who restores furniture professionally. Like most strong chemicals they can be extremely dangerous if used carelessly and you should take great care to protect yourself and your clothing while using them. Above all keep children and pets well out of the way. Even domestic bleach can be very dangerous and should be kept locked away when not in use.

Apply domestic or wood bleach neat to the wood with a brush, give it time to work and then wash it off thoroughly and give the wood plenty of time to dry before doing anything more. If you buy one of the other bleaches in crystal form be sure to reconstitute it by adding the crystals to the water and not the other way round. This will help to minimise fumes. After these bleaches have had time to work they should also be rinsed off with generous amounts of water and left to dry.

When it has been stripped, sanded and bleached your furniture is ready to take its new finish. When choosing a finish (see p. 41) remember that it is not just the appearance of the furniture which matters. The finish is also a *protection* for the wood, and the more wear and tear it is subjected to the more important it is to choose a hard-wearing finish that will not need constant repair.

Treating and preventing insect infestation

Woodworm (furniture beetle)

The life-cycle of the woodworm covers a span of three or four years from the time a beetle lays its eggs on the wood to the time when the new beetle hatches out and emerges from the wood in the early summer, leaving behind it the tell-tale woodworm hole which is the obvious sign of infestation. In the meantime the grubs have been boring their way undetected through the wood, weakening it considerably. An additional sign of infestation is a fine powder which falls out if the furniture is tapped sharply. Woodworm can usually be effectively treated so there is no need to cut away affected wood and replace it, unless the structure has been so substantially weakened that it is no longer serviceable.

Proprietary vermifuges are available with applicators which enable you to inject the liquid right into the woodworm holes and into the wood. In addition to injecting the liquid you should brush over the entire surface of the infected wood. (Test on a hidden area in case the liquid discolours the wood permanently.) If you are using an aerosol spray protect your eyes as the liquid may rebound against the wood. Use rubber gloves and wherever possible work out of doors.

If this is not possible protect the floor and make sure the room is well ventilated. Repeat treatments at least once. The holes can be left or camouflaged by filling with plastic wood or any proprietary wood filler in a matching shade. Overfill slightly and sand smooth when dry. If the wood surface is very noticeable, finish with a more accurately matched stain and polish. Filling the holes enables you to see whether infestation is continuing if any new holes appear after treatment.

Fumigating books

Old books may be attacked by insects such as woodworm, silver fish and booklice, particularly if they have been left undisturbed for a long time in damp conditions or in closed bookshelves where fresh air cannot circulate. Prevent infestation by frequent dusting and by making sure that the books are not jammed tightly together where the air cannot get at them. Infestation can be halted by fumigating the books. After fumigation they should be put in a well ventilated room to allow the fumes to clear.

To fumigate, place the books in an airtight box lined with cotton wool which has been well sprinkled with carbon disulphide or para-dichlorobenzene crystals or sprayed with a proprietary vermifuge. Place more of the treated cotton wool over the book before closing the box. Leave undisturbed for at least twenty-four hours. Repeat the treatment at least once after an interval of twenty-one days.

Natural finishes

Natural finishes have become very popular. 'Natural' does not necessarily mean that you leave the wood its natural colour, although many people like to do so. It really means that you avoid disguising the wood with thick lacquers and paints and rely on the natural grain and appearance of the wood to create an attractive piece of furniture. The most 'natural' natural finishes are achieved by using the traditional methods, oiling and waxing. However a similar effect can be achieved with modern lacquers, including polyurethanes. Remember that your choice of finish depends on the amount and type of wear the furniture will be getting as well as its appearance. You may decide that a hard-wearing heat and water resistant polyurethane is more practical for your purposes than an oiled finish which is easily marked.

Staining and colouring

Staining wood does not have to be a complicated business unless you want it to be. Many specialist books give traditional recipes for wood stains, which are fun to make if you are determined to give your furniture a totally traditional finish, but which are now largely obsolete unless you are dealing with very high quality hardwoods for first class cabinet work. You can give a good quality finish to your work by using ready mixed proprietary wood stains, available from DIY shops and woodwork shops. The matt variety is almost always the type to use. These stains are given the names of the types of wood to which they approximate, but the names are only intended as a rough guide and the stains can be mixed to give innumerable variations. The final colour of your furniture will also depend on the colour of the wood itself, whether or not you have bleached it, how far the stain penetrates and the type of sealer or lacquer you use on top of it. You do not have to confine yourself to traditional colours. Brightly coloured dyes can be used in conjunction with protective finishes (see Modern lacquers). You may decide not to use a stain at all but to rely on a combination of the original wood colour and the sealer.

Matt wood stains are usually a better choice than the coloured polyurethane lacquers which are also marketed under the names of different wood types, but which can cause a build up of colour (see Modern lacquers). Whatever your choice, be sure to try it out on a concealed area before applying it to the entire piece of furniture. Allow the stain to dry, and seal it as you intend to, to get a true idea of the final effect.

Most stains are suitable for use under sealers like oil, wax, French polish and any brand of modern lacquer. However the intensity of a colour can be affected, and if you are using a synthetic lacquer it is best wherever possible to use a stain made by the same manufacturer. Obviously stain should be applied according to the manufacturer's instructions. This usually means using a large soft brush to give the surface as even an application as possible and then using a clean, dry cloth to wipe up any excess stain before it dries patchily. If a water-based stain raises the grain of the wood it must be rubbed down before sealer or lacquer is applied.

Oiled finishes

Oiling, even in conjunction with waxing, produces a gentle matt finish. It prevents dirt getting into the wood, but does not give much protection against heat. The best oil to use is either linseed oil (boiled or raw, boiled is thicker) or teak oil. Teak oil is quicker drying than linseed oil and does not mark quite so easily. There are also several proprietary brands of oil which are marketed for this purpose. Oiling will inevitably darken the wood, although you can minimise the darkening effects of linseed oil (boiled or raw) by diluting it with as much as 50 per cent white spirit. If you are working on a newly stripped surface you may want to alter the basic colour of the wood with a matt wood stain (see Staining and colouring). Always try the stain on a hidden surface before going ahead with the final application. Apply the oil in several thin coats rather than one drenching, as this will give a more even appearance and prevent over-darkening the wood. Allow the wood to dry for 6–8 hours between coats. Continue the applications until the wood can absorb no more oil, then rub away any excess oil with a clean soft rag.

An oiled finish can be left as it is or can be waxed with a good quality wax polish. This adds to its sheen and provides greater protection for the wood. The first application of wax after oiling should be done with a very fine (grade 000) steel wool. After that polish the furniture in the usual way. Where oiled furniture is dull but otherwise sound you can revitalise the finish and preserve the patina by removing accumulated layers of old wax with methylated spirit or white spirit and steel wool, resealing with a fresh application of oil, and repolishing.

Waxed finishes

Wax gives additional protection and lustre to wood which has already been treated with other finishes such as French polish. However if you have not already applied another finish, but want to use wax alone to give a natural finish to wood which has been stripped of its original finish, the wood must first be sealed. There is no need to use a grain filler but the colour of the wood can be changed with matt wood stain if desired. You can seal the wood with oil (see above) but this will give a matt effect. Other sealers are transparent French polish, which is shellac based (two or three thin coats applied with a brush and rubbed down with a medium fine grade of sandpaper to give the wax a good surface to adhere to), or a modern wood sealer, which is usually polyurethane based. A good quality hard white wax, ideally one made with beeswax, should then be applied and worked into the wood with fine wire wool. Several applications, well polished, are far better than one thick, smeary layer. Periodically inspect waxed furniture and, if it has become dull and grubby, clean off wax with methylated spirit or white spirit and rewax. If you have a power tool with a polishing attachment you can quickly build up the sort of patina which used to take years of hard work by hand.

If you like doing as much as possible in the traditional craftsman's way, you can make your own furniture polish. There are many recipes for polish, all variations on the same theme. Remember when you buy beeswax that the yellow type will slightly alter the colour of wood. The best quality polishes use white beeswax, which is slightly more expensive.

Homemade beeswax polish

Half fill a watertight container with beeswax and melt it gently by placing it in a bowl of hot water. When the wax is melted add an equal quantity of real turpentine (not white spirit). Blend the two ingredients thoroughly. Store the polish tightly covered or it will quickly dry out.

Modern lacquers

You can save a lot of time and hard work by finishing wood with a modern synthetic lacquer. These are usually sold in matt, gloss or satin finishes. A synthetic gloss will give a very high intensity polish. You can make your own satin lacquer by mixing gloss and matt together. If you like the colour of the wood a transparent lacquer can be applied directly to the surface, although it will probably darken the appearance a little. Many modern wood lacquers are polyurethanes. These lacquers have a very good resistance to heat, moisture and dirt, but *only if they are applied direct to the wood or another polyurethane finish*. They do not penetrate the wood, so you must be sure to prepare the wood by sanding down first. Apply several coats, rubbing down with steel wool in between coats.

Transparent modern wood lacquers, including those which are polyurethane-based, can be applied over a wood stain, if you want to change the colour of the wood. By using a matt wood stain and then giving it a protective seal of clear varnish you can control the colour of the wood. It is possible to buy polyurethane lacquers which colour as they seal the wood. The disadvantage of these is that because they do not soak into the wood the colour builds up with each application, so that to get a tough finish you may find you end up with a much darker colour than you intended, and the natural appearance of the wood grain may be obscured.

If you want to give wood a non-wood colour and yet keep the added attraction of the wood's texture, use modern lacquers over the brightly coloured wood stains which are now available. Bright colours are available in polyurethane lacquers as well as wood stains, and again caution must be used against a build-up of over-concentrated colour. It is probably best to use a clear polyurethane lacquer over an ordinary stain. You can of course experiment with other forms of colouring, such as fabric dyes or watercolours, which can then be protected by transparent lacquer. You may find these tend to go pale when dry so make the colours a little stronger than they are intended to be. Do not forget that colours do not have to be painted in a uniform way over the wood surface. They can be used to draw patterns and pictures on to the wood. For example, you could make a chess table by marking out squares in different colours, or you could paint an imitation of inlaid work on to a plain surface. The design should then be protected by several coats of clear polyurethane.

French polishing

French polish gives a hard, glossy appearance, but is easily damaged by heat and moisture and so is not suitable for very utilitarian furniture. The polish itself is made up of shellac and methylated spirit. You can mix this yourself, but proprietary brands are easily obtainable and make French polishing a comparatively simple business.

Having stripped and sanded down furniture to a smooth surface you will have to fill the grain with a *grain filler* so that the French polish does not look uneven because it has been absorbed more deeply by some pores than by others. Standard wood stopping thinned with turpentine and tinted with powdercolour to match the wood can be used as a grainfiller, but it is best wherever possible to use a product made by the same manufacturer as the French polish. This applies to the wood stain as well if you are using one to change the wood colour. This means that you can confidently mix the stain and the filler together, knowing that they are intended to be complementary. The job of staining and filling can then be done in one go. Use a proprietary matt wood stain available from DIY shops or woodworker supply shops. Whether you are mixing it with filler or not, the stain you have chosen should be tested on a hidden surface before use so that you can see what the final colour will look like. Colour names like oak, mahogany and walnut are only approximate. You may find you get the exact shade you want by mixing several colours together.

Staining is not always necessary if you are French polishing as the polish comes in half a dozen standard colours as well as transparent. Use the transparent type if you have already used a stain or if you want to retain the natural colour of the wood.

When the surface has been prepared by filling and colouring give it time to dry (overnight is usually sufficient) before applying polish. There are several brands of ready mixed French polish to choose from. Use a modern one based on polyurethane if you want to polish over a polyurethane stain.

This type cannot be used to touch up damaged standard French polish without losing its heat and water resisting properties. The manufacturer's notes should make it possible for you to decide which brand of polish is best for the wood you are treating. One or two polishes are marketed with a special finish which can be used as a final application to remove the smear marks, which are a common problem on amateur French polishing.

Another common problem is that of dust sticking to the polish. The polish dries very quickly but even so the surface will attract dust unless you take great care to make the surroundings as clean as possible. Dampening the floor will help reduce dust.

Follow the manufacturer's instructions when applying the polish. Some recommend you to make the initial covering with a brush, but apart from this the basic polishing movement should either be circular or in a figure of eight. The polish should be applied on a pad made up by wrapping wadding or cotton wool in a fluff-free rag such as a well washed cotton handkerchief. Open up the rag and saturate the wadding or cotton wool with polish, then wrap the rag round the saturated wadding and twist the ends together. The polish can then be released in small quantities by squeezing the pad gently as you work over the wood. Replenish the wad with polish as necessary. The polish should be allowed to dry between coats and then rubbed down lightly with very fine grade wire wool. This is particularly important when the first layers of polish are applied, as the moisture may raise the grain of the wood. Each layer should be slightly thinner than the last, methylated spirit being used to dilute it. It is up to you how many layers you use, but the final polish should be mainly methylated spirit, which will evaporate and leave a very thin, shiny layer of polish.

Use a fresh pad for the final layers of polish, and if it seems to be 'catching' a lot, put a few drops of linseed oil on to the pad.

Do *not* use *any* oil for the *final* application of polish. Make up a completely fresh polishing pad if necessary.

French polish should be wax polished to preserve its appearance.

Painted finishes

It is best to use paint on imperfect wood surfaces, rather than to cover up attractively textured wood. If you have patched up wood with plastic wood or filler or if stripping reveals that someone else has done the same thing before you, then an opaque, painted finish is obviously more sensible than a lighter finish such as oil or wax. Paint is also a good finish for furniture used by children as it is resistant to most spills, except strong alcohol which acts as a solvent; marks are easily wiped off. Use paint too if you want to give a uniform finish to several items of furniture to make a set. A plain colour is easiest and a simple finish is often the most effective, but ideas and methods are given for several decorative ways with painted finishes. A simple but effective technique is to use a different shade of the same basic colour in panels or on drawer fronts.

Preparing the wood

Remove all metal fittings before you begin and clean them separately (see p. 134). Removable fittings should be replaced when painting is complete.

The most thorough preparation is to strip right down to the bare wood with a paint remover and sand paper (see Cleaning and removing old finishes from wood) and then use a filler. You can choose from several fillers marketed specifically for use before painting, and it is probably best to use one of the same make as the paint you are using. Large blemishes should be filled with plastic wood and knot holes sealed with knotting solution. The surface should feel smooth when you run your fingers across it.

If you decide in advance to use a paint finish you can save yourself a lot of work simply by making good the original surface rather than stripping and sanding completely. In this case make sure the surface is thoroughly clean and dry. Remove with methylated spirit or white spirit any wax or oil which might prevent the paint from adhering. Fill large blemishes and, when the filler is dry, sand roughly so that excess filler and any of the old finish which is loose or flakey is removed. Brush away the dust and run your fingers over the surface to check that there are no lumps and bumps.

Continue the making-good process by going over the surface with a proprietary spackle (extra-fine filler) which should be taken over the old finish as well as any bare wood. Finally go over the surface with fine sandpaper, and dust well before painting.

Brushes

It pays to use good quality brushes as these give better cover with each brush stroke, are less likely to leave fine lines in the painted finish and shed fewer hairs. You will do a better job if you also check that the brush is comfortable to hold. Before using a new brush take the trouble to work the bristles across the palm of your hand and to twirl the handle rapidly between the palms of your hands (diagrams 1a and 1b) so that any loose hairs work their way out before they get trapped in your paintwork. Some people condition *natural bristle* brushes before using them by soaking them overnight in linseed oil. Do not do this if the brush is going to be used for French polish and it is a waste of time to do this to synthetic fibre brushes. If you do decide to give your brush this treatment make sure that all traces of linseed oil are removed with turpentine or white spirit before you use it for painting.

When you have finished painting make sure that your brushes are

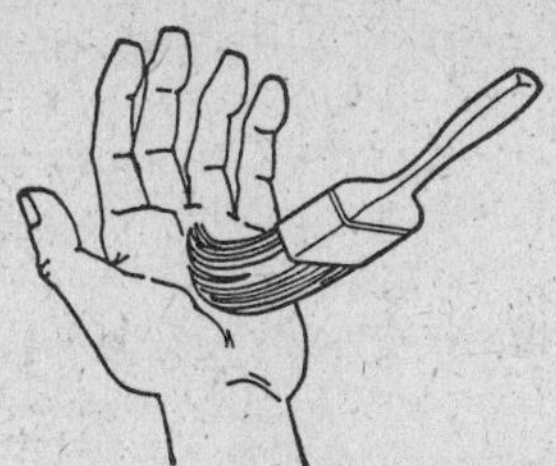
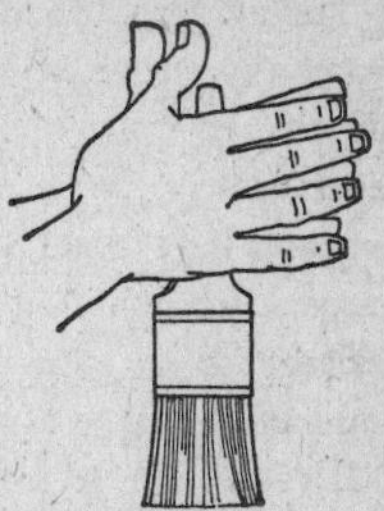

DIAGRAMS 1a and b
Work loose hairs out of brush before painting

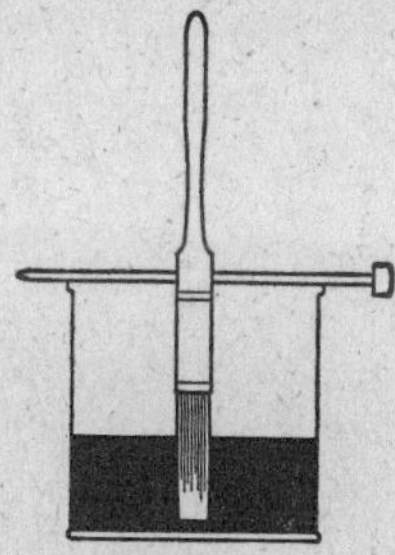

DIAGRAM 2
Suspend brush on paint tin to prevent bristles bending

clean before storing them. If you are only halting temporarily wrap the brush tightly in aluminium foil. Otherwise remove all traces of paint. Water-based paints (look at the tin) will wash off with detergent and water. Other paints, and that means most gloss paints, should be cleaned off with proprietary paint remover or white spirit before washing. French polish will come off with methylated spirit. Hang the brush on a nail or store it flat until it dries out then wrap the bristles in brown paper and store flat or hanging from a nail. A brush left for a short time should not be allowed to stand on its bristles so that they become bent. Instead run something like a knitting needle through the hole in the handle and suspend the brush across the tin or jar that you are using (diagram 2).

Painting

Once the wood surface has been cleaned ready for painting, conditions should be kept as clean as possible – dust, fluff and sawdust will adhere to the paint while it is drying and spoil the surface. Many paints are inflammable and it is wise not to smoke while painting, especially if using a spray paint.

The prepared wood should first be given a coat of *primer*, which will be largely absorbed by the wood. Some undercoats incorporate a primer as well. If, in spite of thorough preparation, the priming coat shows up a mass of small imperfections you should go over the surface again with the finest filler (spackle). The next stage is *undercoating*, with at least two coats, rubbing down with fine glass paper when each coat dries. Because most of the undercoat is absorbed, you get a better quality finish with the top coat which lies smoothly on the surface of the wood. The *topcoats* (usually two although you may decide on more especially if covering an old finish) should be applied as sparingly as possible and each coat, except the final one, should be gently sanded when it dries. Always brush from the uncovered area back to the area you have already covered, in a north/south direction as well as an east/west direction (diagram 3) to avoid brush marks, and work on a horizontal surface wherever possible to prevent drips and runs.

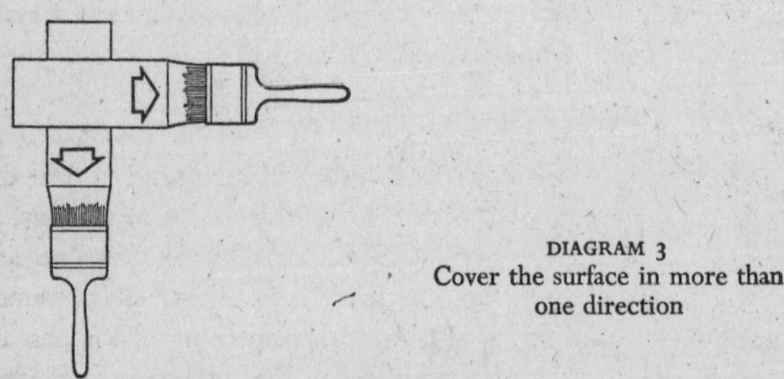

DIAGRAM 3
Cover the surface in more than one direction

Aerosol paints

Aerosol paints can now be obtained in a wide range of colours, and you can buy aerosol primers and undercoats as well as gloss and emulsion. There are aerosol paints for other materials such as metal. They are particularly useful for fiddly jobs like wickerwork. The main point to remember when using them is that they cover a very wide area. If you cannot use them out of doors make sure that clothes, floors and walls are well protected. Do not smoke while using aerosol paints.

Transfers, self-adhesive motifs, stencils and freehand designs

These methods of decorating furniture are usually used on furniture which has already been painted a plain colour. Of course, there is no reason why they should not be used on furniture with a natural finish. If this is what you wish to do it is better to apply transfers, stencils and painted designs onto the wood *before* coating it with a protective layer of clear varnish. Self-adhesive motifs can be applied over almost any finish. You can buy them from most art shops, from which you can also buy transfers, stencils and acrylic paints.

Transfers

Transfers are very thin and this is their advantage over self-adhesive motifs. They come on a water-soluble backing which is soaked off. Once this backing has disappeared the transfer is too fragile to manoeuvre. An old transfer cannot be peeled off but has to be removed with paint remover or glass paper. Transfers should always be protected by a layer of clear lacquer.

Self-adhesive motifs

These can be applied over any finish. Their disadvantage is that they are rather thick compared with the alternatives. Unless they are carefully applied the edges tend to roll up and the adhesive edge attracts dirt and dust. On the other hand it is an easy job to remove them completely and replace them with something else when this happens, or when you grow tired of them. The adhesive mark comes off when rubbed with a little methylated spirit or surgical spirit.

Stencils

These can be bought ready made from art shops or you can make them yourself by cutting patterns with a sharp Stanley knife out of waxed paper or PVC flooring material. However, if you are able to make satisfactory stencils yourself you will probably be able to paint freehand designs for which stencils are usually a substitute. Successful stencil designs depend on the right consistency of paint. This should be thick enough to prevent seepage under the cut-out edges of the pattern, and thin enough not to go tacky and stick to the stencil. A good product for stencils is acrylic paint, which comes in tubes and which can be thinned with water to the desired consistency. As with most painting, it is helpful to turn the furniture so that you are working on a horizontal surface, particularly as you will need to keep the stencil still while you are applying the paint. You will have better control over the paint if you use a fairly stiff brush. You should fix the stencil securely in place while you are working with it. It is possible to cut stencils from PVC material with a self-adhesive backing, the type of material used to line shelves and drawers. Although this makes securing the stencil while you work a comparatively easy matter, you may find you are left with marks from the adhesive, or worse still that part of the base finish comes away with the stencil.

Freehand designs (Advanced)

It will help your attempts at painting pictures onto a plain ground if you choose two strongly contrasting colours to work with. This will allow you to paint the entire surface in a plain colour first and then mark out your design and paint it over the base colour. If you use two similar or two pale colours it is best to mark out the design on the bare wood and paint the background colour round the design, using a very fine brush for the edges adjacent to the area of the picture. For plain geometric designs this should be a sufficient precaution. The design is painted into the remaining space. If the design is complex, paint it in first with a rubber-based masking compound into which you fix a small piece of paper so that it can be pulled off in a piece when you have finished painting the background. This has the additional advantage that it makes it possible to use a spray paint for the base colour. Masking can also be done with self-adhesive PVC. The design is traced onto the back, cut out and applied to the wood before the background is painted. The disadvantages are described under Stencils. Whichever way you decide to work it is always essential to allow the base paint several days to dry really thoroughly. It is usually easiest not to draw your original design direct onto the wood but to draw it on paper, take a tracing, and then trace the copy onto the wood. You can, of course, trace any pattern, not necessarily your own design. Wallpaper pattern books are a good source of designs, especially if you are thinking in terms of repeating a traditional pattern. There is an unending source of pictures to be had from book illustrations. The simpler the design the more successful it is likely to be.

The diagrams (1a and 1b) show how you can enlarge or reduce designs taken from other sources by using squared paper. It is important to adjust the size of a design to fit in with the proportions of the furniture. Diagrams 2–4 give some examples of traditional patterns which you can either use directly or adapt to your own requirements.

DIAGRAM 1a
Draw a grid of squares over original design

DIAGRAM 1b
Reduce design by drawing a grid of smaller squares onto surface and copying the design square by square

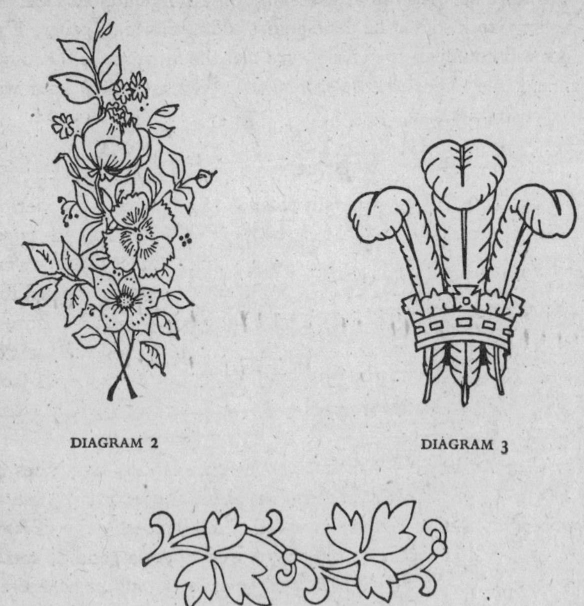

DIAGRAM 2

DIAGRAM 3

DIAGRAM 4
Repeat motif

Fabric and wallpaper on furniture

This is a way of making plain furniture more interesting. The variations are endless: panels in furniture covered to match the wallpaper of the room, contrasting plain fabric to line a display case, printed velvet under glass to restore a damaged table top—these are just a few of the possibilities. Fabric and wallpaper decoration can be used inside furniture as well as outside. In fact, you may find this a useful way of disguising a badly finished interior or of lightening the interior of a gloomy wardrobe. Since you are dealing with relatively small areas, you should be able to buy oddments of very good quality wallpaper (washable vinyl is most practical) at good prices.

Whether you are working with fabric or paper it is best to turn the furniture so that you are working on a horizontal surface. Any refinishing work should be done before adding fabric or paper. If you are not refinishing all over make sure that the furniture is thoroughly clean and free of dust before you begin or you may mark your work with dirty fingers.

Using fabric

There are some fabrics, generally intended for use as wall coverings, which have a special lining that can be glued directly to wood. In general, however, it is better when working with materials to make a card shape of the area you wish to cover and fix the material round that. For large areas plywood may be a better support. The fabric-covered card can then be secured in position with drawing pins or upholstery pins with attractive brass heads. Even if you are using a wall fabric this may be a better idea, as cleaning and replacement are much easier with this method than unsticking a large area of fabric.

Try to avoid fabric which frays easily. Felt is ideal as it does not fray at all. To get a really professional finish the trick is to use adhesive only on the back of the card and to fold an inch or so of fabric round the back of the card, mitreing edges to get a good fit and to avoid lumpiness (diagrams 1 and 2). Almost any type of adhesive is

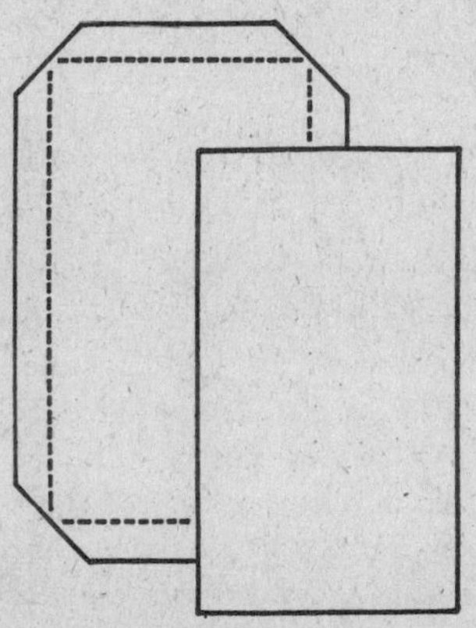

DIAGRAM 1
Fold fabric round card. Mitre edges

DIAGRAM 2
Stick fabric to back of card only

suitable (check the manufacturer's instructions) but they all tend to yellow with age so be sure not to let any seep round to the front of the card and through the fabric.

To make an accurate shape to fix to the wood, begin by making a template (pattern) out of brown paper (diagram 3). Measure the area as accurately as possible and fold the template to that size. Then fit the template against the surface to be covered and make final adjustments to get a really accurate fit. This is a particularly valuable precaution with old furniture which rarely has straight sides and perfect right angles. Use this accurate template to measure out the backing card. For the most accurate results cut this card using a sharp Stanley knife rather than scissors. Place the card horizontally on a flat surface which cannot be damaged by the knife (diagram 4). The fabric itself should be cut larger to allow for fitting round the card.

DIAGRAM 3
Make a paper template of area to be covered

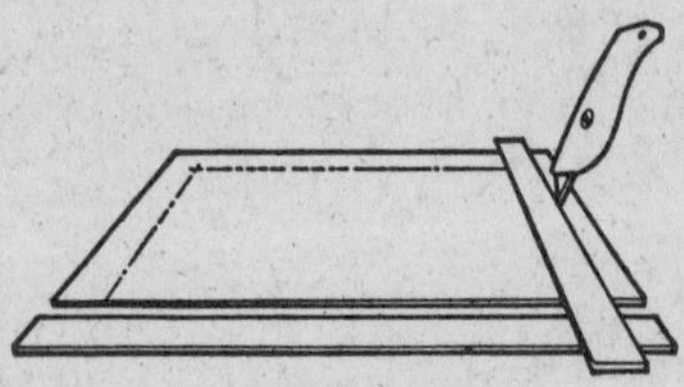

DIAGRAM 4
Cut card to size and shape of template with a Stanley knife

Using paper

Make a template (see above) of the area you wish to cover and use this to mark out the shape on the back of the paper. Allow a little extra for final adjustments. Paper can be stuck directly onto the wood surface. An adhesive which is intended for use with paper and wood (check manufacturer's instructions) is probably better than wallpaper paste. The important point to remember is to use adhesive all over the area but to use it sparingly, so that seepage does not mark the surface of the paper itself.

Antiquing and fake finishes on wood (Advanced)

'Antiquing' is the term used for reproducing the effect of early painted furniture, which used to be the only alternative to a waxed finish before the 1830's when French polish became possible and popular. The aim is to make furniture look as if it were painted in that period, and although the effect is achieved with paint it is intended to imitate a finish which is far superior to the sort of furniture which we now associate with paint. Nowadays paint is used to cover up wood which is not really attractive in its own right, and variations on painted furniture tend towards the cheerful and folksy. Ideas and methods for this type of finish are given on page 51. However much good quality old furniture used to be finished with paint, but with more subtle colours and designs. For example, paint would be used to imitate the bamboo which was so popular as part of the interest in Chinese furniture at the end of the eighteenth century. When 'antiquing' furniture, therefore, the aim is to create an impression of paint which has mellowed with age and where some decoration has remained intact despite wear and tear. The overall effect is restrained and down-beat. You can get ideas by looking at pieces in museums. Any or all of the following methods can then be used to imitate the originals.

1. The simplest way to achieve the effect of 'antique' painted furniture is to choose one of the typical shades used and to add decoration in the correct style. Typical colours are pastel shades such as jade green, deep pink and grey, and stronger colours such as olive green, rust and Chinese lacquer red. Variations on white, often with

grey or cream overtones, were also popular and allow for a great deal of choice in the colour of the decoration. Either a gloss or matt finish can be used but a matt shade is more subtle and usually makes it easier to get the right effect. Typical decoration, in a toning or contrasting colour, or in a gold paint, is a thin line following a feature of the furniture, just within the edge of a panel or chair back for example. A double line, in the same colour or a slight variation of the same colour, is another possibility. A thin gold line on a painted wooden handle is a typical feature. With practice you can paint imitation bamboo or inlay. Some ideas are given in diagrams 1–5. The decoration should be done with thin art brushes. Use artists' oil paints; these can be thinned to the right shade and consistency with a mixture of turpentine and raw linseed oil. However this would not be very hard-wearing without a protective varnish, and it may not be

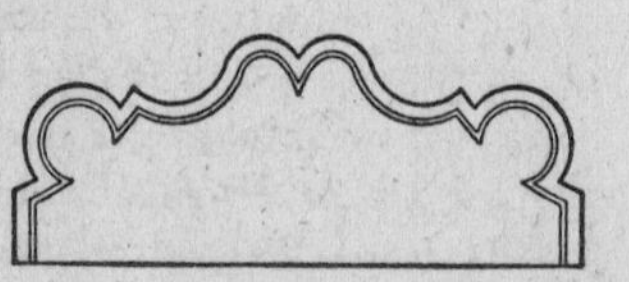

DIAGRAM 1 and 2
A single or double line following the shape of the wood creates the right 'antique' effect

DIAGRAM 3 and 4
Typical inlay designs which can be imitated by 'antiquing'

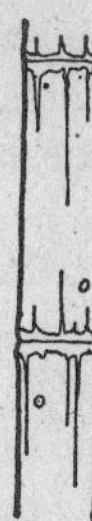

DIAGRAM 5
Imitating bamboo

easy to varnish only over the area of decoration. An alternative method is to mix the oil colour with turpentine and a matt polyurethane varnish so that the decoration and protection can be done in one operation.

2. Another simple way to achieve an 'antique' painted effect is to use two different shades of the same colour as the final two topcoats when painting furniture (usually the light shade over the dark) and then to abrade gently so that the underlying colour shows in a random fashion all over the piece. Choose two shades of one of the typical 'antique' colours. Use the finest grade of steel wool to abrade the top coat and work along the natural line of the furniture. The final effect should be of subtle stripes of colour which vary according to the light. Since you are trying to give an impression of paintwork which has worn and mellowed with age, it would be better to leave lighter the areas such as the arms of chairs, which would have received most wear. You can add to the effect by adding a little simple decoration in a constrasting or toning colour or in imitation gilding (see 1. above). Remember all the time to keep everything a little less than perfect and brand-new looking. As your skill increases you may like to experiment with three or more shades of the same colour.

3. A third method of 'antiquing' furniture, which can be used alone or in combination with either of the other two methods, is to cover paint with a varnish wash, which is then partially wiped away so that the base colour shows through in varying degrees of intensity. In the United States, where 'antique' painted furniture is particularly popular, the varnish/glaze can be bought in special kits, often with a complementary *protective varnish*. If you cannot buy one of these kits a clear polyurethane varnish can be substituted for the protective

finish, if you think the furniture you are dealing with will be subject to hard wear. For the *antiquing varnish/glaze* make up a mixture similar to the one used for adding fine decoration (see 1. above); that is, approximately 1 part artist's oil colour to 1 part raw linseed oil and 3 parts turpentine. The oil colours used are normally variations of brown—the darker the base paint you are glazing, the darker the brown colour you should use in the glaze. So for pale colours choose a shade like umber. Slightly darker is burnt sienna, while raw sienna gives a brownish yellow tone. For really dark colours use black oil paint in the glaze. A slightly less authentic result is achieved by using an oil colour which tones or contrasts with the base paint.

Paint the glaze on with a wide, soft brush. The longer the glaze is left on, the darker and more ageing the effect it will give. An average time to leave it on is about 15 minutes, by which time it starts to go dull. Now wipe away the glaze, using a clean fluff-free rag and removing as little or as much glaze as you want to create the desired effect. The results will be more convincing if you remove more glaze from the areas which would normally have received most wear.

Fake finishes

Apply the base coat and glaze as for antiquing method 3, but make sure your combination of colours fits in with the type of effect you want to achieve; for example, a white base with a black glaze would give a satisfactory marbled appearance. Experience will show you what effects you can copy and how to achieve them. A copy of *wood grain* can be achieved by using a very fine dry brush on the wet glaze (diagram 6). Marble is imitated by placing a large sheet of crumpled brown paper or plastic onto the freshly painted surface of the object, leaving it for a minute and then removing it without smudging. Wiping the glaze with different textures such as carpet or sponge will create interesting patterns. So too will combing through the paint or spattering the glaze with a brush dipped in turpentine.

DIAGRAM 6
Wood grain patterns can be 'faked' with paint

Découpage (Advanced)

Découpage is the craft of decorating with cut-out paper pictures. It is a very old art dating from at least the eighteenth century, when it was used for decorating fans with paper patterns to imitate real lace. However, it is particularly associated with the Victorian era, when découpage was applied to a wide variety of objects and it became fashionable to use cut-out pictures rather than plain paper. It can be used on almost any surface but is most effective on glass or small items of wooden furniture.

On wood

The simplest way of using découpage is to apply cut-out pictures to a plain painted surface and seal them with a coat of clear varnish. This can be very effective. However to do the job properly is a little more complex, as really successful découpage tends to have a look of depth which is acquired by applying many coats of varnish. If used over an unusual finish such as a coloured or stippled stain you can give a very dull piece of furniture the attractive folksy look of an old decorated sea box or cottage blanket chest.

The first consideration is to choose a selection of pictures which match the type of furniture you are trying to create. For example, pictures cut from a flower catalogue would be a good choice for cottage style furniture.

The next point to consider is how to cut out the pictures. Practice helps here and it is better not to choose designs which require cutting from the centre as well as the edges until you have built up a good deal of skill. Use a pair of nail or embroidery scissors with a short blade, so that you have the maximum control over what you are doing. If you use a pair with a curved blade (hold the curved side away from you) you will have the additional advantage of getting a picture where the top surface is fractionally longer than the underside, so that the edges of the picture will lie almost completely flat to the surface when it is glued down.

The surface to which you are applying the cut-outs should be properly prepared *i.e.* smooth and clean. Decide *before* you begin sticking the pictures down where you want them to go. Only start glueing when you are completely satisfied with the design. A water-soluble glue is best, because you can then easily wipe away any glue which oozes out from under the picture. Check the information on the packet to make sure you get the right type of glue. When applying the cut-outs you may find a small sponge or roller useful. Even if you simply use your fingers, apply pressure from the centre to the edges so that you do not end up with a bubble of air or glue in the centre.

When the glue is dry, seal the pictures and the wood with a coat of clear French polish (shellac and methylated spirit), allow to dry, then rub down very, very lightly with finest grade steel wool. After this apply a coat of clear lacquer. From now on it is up to you how many coats of varnish you have the patience to apply, but you will need at least half a dozen to give the impression that the découpage is an integral part of the wood. The surface should feel smooth to your fingers, with no raised edges. Once the surface feels sufficiently smooth, there is no danger of tearing the pictures if you rub down gently between further coats of varnish. Use dampened glass paper of the 'wet and dry' type. This will prevent the abrasive action from being too drastic. When you have applied as many coats of varnish as you think necessary (make sure you let each application dry thoroughly before applying the next) you can finish off with an application of a good quality white wax polish.

On glass

Découpage is a traditional form of decoration for old glass jars and bottles which can be transformed into lamp bases *etc*. You can simply apply the cut-outs to the outside of the glass and give a coat of clear varnish. It is more difficult but also more satisfactory to apply the cut-outs to the interior of the container. To begin with it is easier to use containers with wide necks, as positioning the pictures can be a very fiddly job. A thin layer of adhesive must be applied to the *surface* of the picture and then it must be manoeuvred with a makeshift tool such as a thin piece of wire. Applying pressure to the pictures so that every bit sticks to the glass is not simple, especially on a curved surface. You will probably have to improvise some sort of pad on the end of a stick or knitting needle so that you can rub gently over the paper (diagram 1). If the glass is a good colour you may be happy to leave it at that. Otherwise you can paint the inside of the glass so that the découpage stands out against a clear background.

DIAGRAM I
Improvise a pad on a long knitting needle to press down designs on interior of jar

Wait until you are sure that the glue is completely dry and all the pictures are secure. Then pour emulsion paint into the container and swirl it around so that all the uncovered glass is covered. Pour out the excess paint and leave to dry. For converting the bottle into a lamp, see p. 137.

5

Paper, prints, books and frames

Paper, prints and books

You can avoid a lot of unnecessary trouble with items made of paper, and that includes books of course, by taking a little care over the conditions in which they are kept. Central heating and air conditioning usually make the air too dry (not necessarily too hot) for paper. The paper will dry out and get brittle. Counteract the dryness with an electric humidifier if possible, or at least by hiding dishes of water under furniture. It will also help if you introduce central heating gradually, increasing the temperature a little at a time over a couple of weeks rather than all at once. This gives your possessions a little time to adjust and is just as important for wooden furniture which is liable to split in sudden extremes of temperature and humidity.

The other extreme, dampness, is also harmful to items made of paper. It encourages mildew, the brown staining known as 'foxing', and certain types of insects. Whatever the conditions it is important to keep fresh air circulating and to dust frequently, including behind pictures. This will discourage insect pests and fungus growths which flourish best when left undisturbed.

Cleaning

Erasing is the simplest method of removing superficial marks and grease. Do not use a harsh rubber. Either use an artist's gum eraser, which is extremely soft, or use soft, fresh, white breadcrumbs. These last are particularly effective if there is any grease in the marks, as they will absorb it. Rub the bread gently over the mark, replacing it with a clean piece as soon as it begins to look dirty.

Stubborn grease marks can be blotted up. Dampen lightly round the edges of the stain to prevent it spreading when melted. Place the paper between two sheets of clean white blotting paper (diagram 1) and iron with a warm iron placed very gently on the blotting paper. Remove the blotting paper immediately it has soaked up any of the warmed grease mark. Repeat with fresh blotting paper if necessary. This method works well on wax. Scrape excess wax off the top of the paper before ironing up the remainder.

DIAGRAM 1
Remove grease marks by placing paper between sheets of blotting paper and applying a warm iron

Greasy marks which do not respond to this treatment can sometimes be removed with a grease solvent. Choose from the list of solvents on p. 147. The solvent should be applied very sparingly on a pad of clean cotton wool. Remember to take adequate precautions for solvents which are inflammable or which have potentially dangerous fumes. If using this method on a book page, make sure the page underneath is protected by something waterproof such as a plastic bag.

Bleach can be used on isolated patches of 'foxing' (the brown staining so frequently found on old paper), on ink marks and on unidentifiable stains. The bleach should be brushed on with a soft brush. As soon as you can see it taking effect, blot it up with clean white blotting paper. Repeat until you think you have removed as much as possible without over-weakening the paper. Brush with distilled water several times to rinse away the bleach, and blot again. For this type of bleaching use hydrogen peroxide or a solution of Chloramine T (1 part Chloramine T to approximately 40 parts distilled water). Household bleach should not be used as it makes the paper too white.

When cleaning book edges by any of the above methods clamp the book tightly (diagram 2) to ensure a firm surface. Bleaches and solvents should be applied on a small pad of cotton wool and wiped off again with a pad of cotton wool rung out in distilled water.

Book pages which have become stuck together should be gently steamed apart (diagram 3). Protect your hands from burns. Interleave the separated pages with sheets of clean, white blotting paper until they are dry and then iron if necessary with a warm iron over brown paper to remove creases.

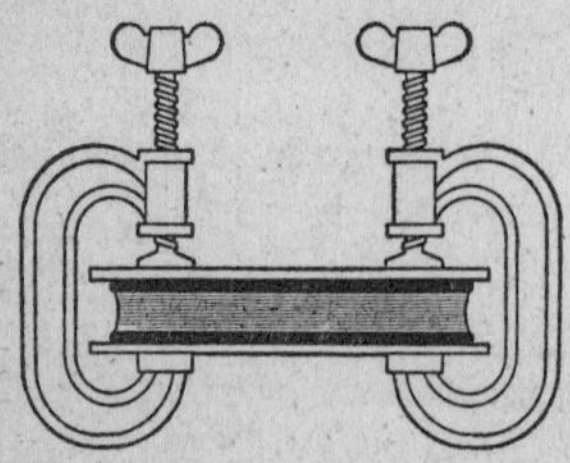

DIAGRAM 2
Clamp book firmly to get a smooth surface on the edges

DIAGRAM 3
Steam pages apart

Cleaning (Advanced)

Extra care is needed when using these methods of soaking paper to clean it, as there is a danger that the paper may disintegrate if carelessly handled.

Make sure that the print you are dealing with is waterproof. Obviously watercolours cannot be given any of these treatments, and many prints will also have been hand-tinted with watercolours which will run if soaked. Some old printers' inks may also run. If you intend to try washing the paper be sure to have plentiful supplies of clean white blotting paper to hand. You will also need a sheet of glass for supporting the paper so that you do not need to handle it while it is wet, and two containers similar to those used by photographers for developing film. Do not place paper in an empty container and then subject it to a jet of water as this may weaken one small area. It is better to slip the paper into a depth of about 3 cm of liquid, and top up the amount if necessary.

Paper which is generally grubby, and particularly prints with remains of old glue adhering to the back, should be immersed in tepid distilled water or distilled water with a small amount of mild detergent added to it (diagram 4). Most of the dirt will float out of the paper unaided, but you can help matters along a little by gently stroking the paper with a soft shaving brush.

DIAGRAM 4
Immerse paper supported on glass sheet

If you use detergent the paper must be immersed in clean distilled water afterwards to 'rinse' it.

After the paper is removed from the liquid, place a piece of clean white blotting paper over it. As soon as this has absorbed the excess moisture, the paper can be slipped onto a pad of several sheets of blotting paper and fresh clean sheets of blotting paper placed on top until it is virtually dry.

Ironing the paper between clean sheets of white blotting paper while it is still just a little damp will get rid of wrinkles.

Too much soaking will eventually remove the size which stiffens the paper, and this will make it floppy. If this happens you can 'resize' the paper by immersing it in a solution of gelatine (15 grammes gelatine to 4½ litres of distilled water). Dry and iron in the usual way.

A bleach solution can be used for soaking prints which are not merely grubby but stained as well. Chloramine T is a good bleach for use on paper. Make up a solution of approximately 1 part Chloramine T to 40 parts distilled water. An alternative is a 5 per cent solution of hydrogen peroxide. Household bleach has too stark an effect and should not be used. Bleaches should be rinsed out with distilled water, although Chloramine T is considered safe to leave in the paper.

Sterilise prints which have been cleaned of foxing and old glue to prevent a re-occurrence of these problems when they are remounted.

Sterilising is done by wiping over the back of the print with a solution of thymol. Fungus can also be discouraged by remounting the print with a synthetic glue as used by photographers for mounting photographic prints.

Mending

Clear Sellotape is the obvious way of mending tears in paper and prints. This should be applied to the wrong side of a print. If there are many tears in a book Sellotape will not be satisfactory because it is fairly thick and, if used too often, will prevent the book from lying flat. You should be able to find an alternative in an artists' supply shop, in the form of thin transparent paper which has to be dampened to make it stick. This has the additional advantage that it does not have a yellowy tinge.

Another, more professional, method of repairing paper, which is not possible if the tear goes over print in a book, but which can be used on the back of a torn print, is to make your own strips of gummed paper. Do this by cutting strips of paper which match the original as exactly as possible, and fix them into place with white paste or one of the adhesives used to mount photographic prints.

This paper strip made from matching paper is the ideal way of mending a book where the cover board has come away from the end papers (diagram 5). Otherwise use the strongest type of Sellotape—Sellotape X. Make sure the repair is not too tight—the book should open and close easily without any strain being put on the repair.

DIAGRAM 5
Make sure a repaired cover has enough 'play' to open easily

Worn gilding on book edges can be restored using a gilt paste such as American Treasure Wax. The book should be clamped together (diagram 2) to create as smooth a surface as possible to work on.

Papier Mâché

Papier Mâché is made of pulped paper or layers of paper mixed with glue. Usually it is lacquered, sometimes with as many as 50 layers. Although it seems hard it is a rather vulnerable substance; being brittle, it is inclined to break, and because of its composition it is easily damaged by liquids and by extremes of temperature.

Cleaning

Dust frequently with a clean, soft cloth. If there is dirt on the surface, polish with a cream furniture polish which cleans as it shines. Be sure to apply it sparingly, do not apply any great pressure while polishing, and wipe away any surplus with a clean cloth. Frequent polishing is *not* necessary. Never clean papier mâché with a liquid, especially not with water: the liquid will penetrate the layers of paper and cause the papier mâché to begin to disintegrate and the lacquered surface to lift off. Metal inlay, which is often found on papier mâché articles, should not be cleaned with ordinary liquid metal polish. Use a cloth impregnated with a metal cleaning chemical. These are easily available from most hardware departments.

Repairs

Missing sections of papier mâché can be replaced, and chips and blemishes filled, using the techniques for mending china (see p. 114). Since the repair will have to be painted over, generally with black lacquer, it is possible to do this with plastic wood, which is an easy substance to work with. Alternatively, use a standard china filler such as epoxy adhesive thickened with kaolin powder or titanium dioxide. An epoxy putty such as this can be mixed with powder pigment of the correct colour before you start the repair, although surface retouching will probably still be necessary. Always overfill to allow for shrinkage and make fine adjustments with a fine 'wet and dry' glass paper which has been dampened. Fine grade wire wool may also be used. Apply the filler in layers on large patches, allowing each to dry before applying the next.

Where large sections are missing you will have to build up the new piece over a wire core and stick it into position when dry, using an epoxy adhesive (see China repairs, p. 114). Make the core with a thin brass wire and cover this with several layers of newspaper soaked in wallpaper paste or flour and water paste. When this is quite dry you will have a base on which you can continue to build with plastic wood or epoxy putty. This can be modelled and abraded to the same shape and size as the missing section.

Woodworm may attack papier mâché. This cannot be treated with the usual liquid insecticides. Instead the piece must be fumigated by the method described for books (see p. 41), and using a crystalline vermifuge such as paradichlorobenzene.

Refinishing

If a papier mâché article is sound but the decoration and gilding are wearing a little thin it is best to leave well alone as amateur work may lessen the value of the piece. Where you have repaired a damaged papier mâché article, some refinishing will be necessary to disguise the work. Use the refinishing methods described for china (see p. 127). Like china, the papier mâché will probably require a final coat of clear varnish to achieve the right effect. A good match for the mellow appearance of the original decoration can be achieved by tinting the varnish very, very slightly with a little yellow colour, and by applying several coats, rubbed down gently with fine grade wire wool. This will prevent the shiny, new appearance of the refinished work catching the eye.

Repairing and re-using old frames

The following list gives the order in which you should dismantle, clean, repair and reassemble an old frame. You may not need to go through the whole process, in which case you should follow the instructions for whatever work is necessary. For example, many frames can be simply repaired (section *c*) without being dismantled, and if the frame is clean and in good condition you may only need to take away the protective paper and backing board (section *a*) and replace the existing picture with one of your own choice. If you do dismantle an old frame completely take advantage of the opportunity to clean it thoroughly.

a Dismantle the frame from the back, keeping a careful note of the different component parts. With minor variations the frame will be made up of the pieces shown in the exploded diagram 1, and listed below:

A protective backing of brown paper securely stuck down to keep dirt out of the picture and neaten the frame.

A stiff backing of card or hardboard. This is wedged in position by tacks knocked into the frame at an angle. If the tacks are very rusty

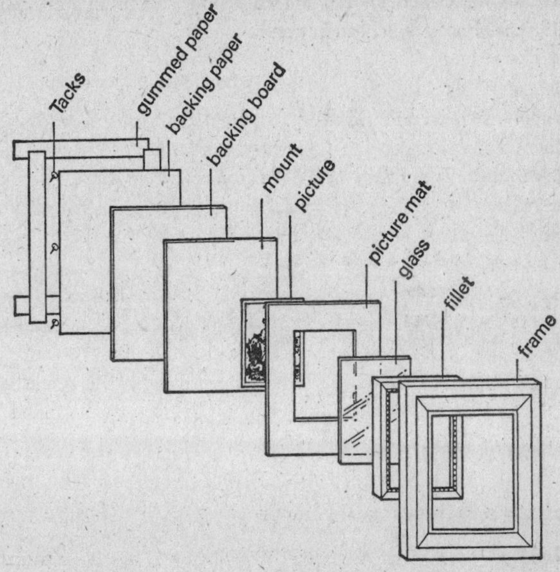

DIAGRAM I

pull them out with pliers and when you replace the backing board, use new tacks knocked into fresh wood at the same angle. The backing board as well as the frame itself should be inspected for woodworm. Treat the frame with a proprietary vermifuge if necessary. It is simpler and more effective to replace an infested piece of backing board than to treat it for woodworm. Wipe the replacement backing card (or board) with a solution of thymol to discourage future fungus growths.

The picture itself mounted on stiff card.

A card 'frame' for the picture (picture mat). If the picture has been carefully mounted on the stiffening card a picture mat may not have been used.

Picture glass which fits into the recesses of the frame itself.

An inner frame (fillet) consisting of four strips of mitred wood which are usually gilded. Like the picture mat, the inner frame is meant to set the picture off to advantage and improve the relative proportions of frame and picture. It is often omitted.

b Clean the components of the frame thoroughly. The wooden frame itself benefits from a good wash in warm, soapy water (be careful not to get it too wet or you may loosen the glue), followed by a polish. Clean the glass with a proprietary window polish, polished off with old newspaper. If you are re-using the original picture and wish to clean it see p. 64, Cleaning paper and prints.

c Repair the frame if necessary. Where the corners of the frame are gaping apart it is probably simplest to repair them with an epoxy adhesive even if nails were used originally. Pull out old nails with pliers, clean old glue off the edges with a solvent (p. 147) and make sure the edges are free of grease by wiping them with methylated spirit. Then glue and clamp the corners together (diagram 2). (For

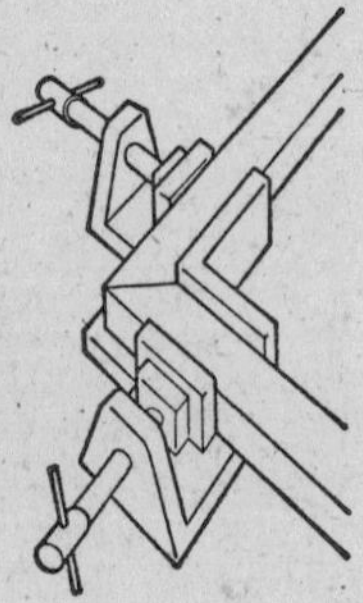

DIAGRAM 2
Clamping mitred corners

more details on repairing wood with adhesive see p. 11.) An alternative repair, and one which may be preferable if you have a very heavy frame, is to reinforce the corners with triangular metal plates fixed to the back of the frame (diagram 3). Screw the plate to the wood; the screw holes are already drilled into the metal plate. Corrugated nails (diagram 4) can be used to draw together mitred corners. Use them by themselves or to strengthen a glued repair. Broken glass should be replaced with *lightweight picture glass*. A glass merchant will cut this to size for you.

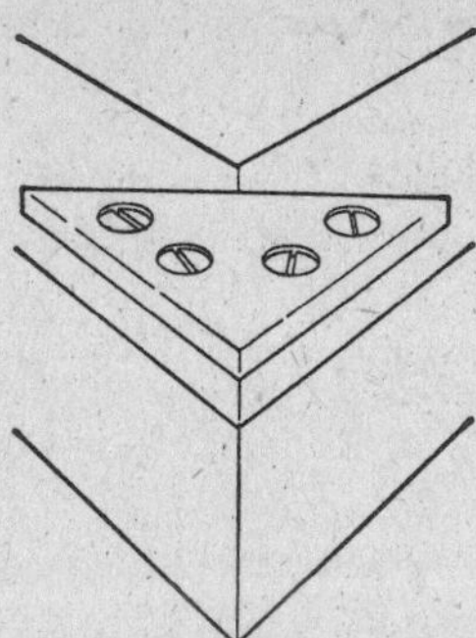

DIAGRAM 3
Reinforcing corners with metal plates

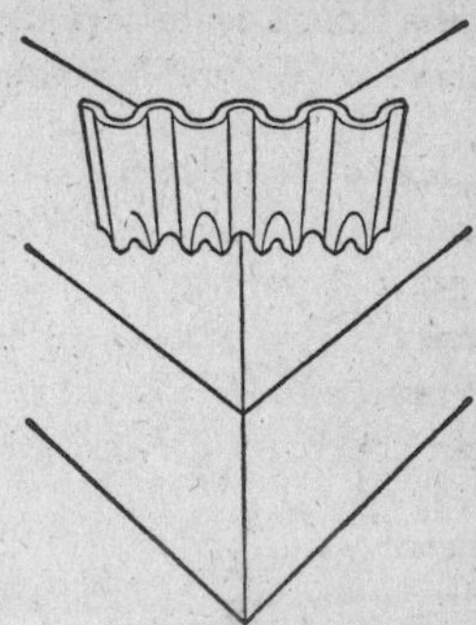

DIAGRAM 4
Reinforcing corners with corrugated nails

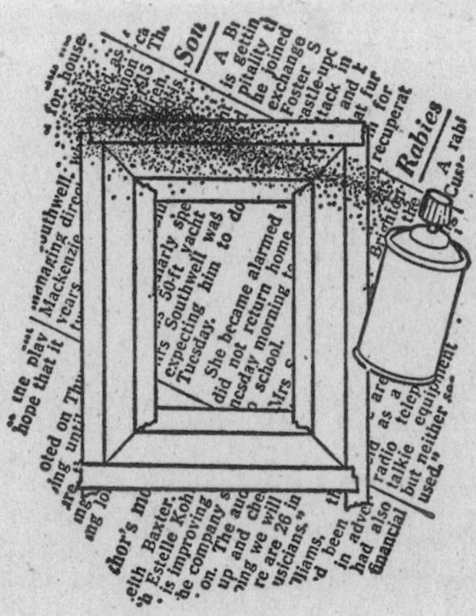

DIAGRAM 5
Mask glass and work-surface when using aerosol paints

d Refinish a wooden frame using the methods described on pages 41–60 for larger items of furniture. If you do not like the existing finish you can sand it off and wax it to get a lighter effect. There are many artificial gold and silver paints, such as the American Treasure

Gold range, which can be used to touch up a gilded frame or to change the colour of a plain wood frame. These artificial gilding preparations can be bought from art shops. If you use an aerosol paint make sure the rest of the frame is masked off (diagram 5). The inner frame is usually gilded and may well need to be given an extra coat of gold paint.

e Remount the picture if the mount has become faded or if the picture has been attacked by fungus and you have cleaned it. Card suitable for mounting pictures is available from art shops. Cut the card so that it fits into the recesses of the frame. If using a picture mat (see below), glue narrow strips of white paper to the edges of the picture and use these to paste the picture to the centre of the card (diagram 6). Leave a little more space below the picture than above it (diagram 7). Use a synthetic adhesive for mounting pictures onto card. This

DIAGRAM 6
The picture is not glued directly to the mount. Narrow strips of paper glued to the print are pasted onto the mount

DIAGRAM 7
Leave more space below the picture

will prevent any fungus growth and 'foxing' which thrives on animal-based glues. Photographic shops stock suitable adhesives. It is best not to apply adhesive directly to the back of the picture itself.

If the mount is to be visible, and you are dispensing with a picture mat, choose a colour card which will set off the picture to advantage. Stick the picture directly to the mount, applying adhesive to the edges of the picture only. Neaten by drawing a double pencil line round the picture.

It is easier to get a more professional look if you make a picture mat to go between the mounted picture and the glass, as small mistakes in centreing and glueing the picture to the backing mount will not show. To make a mat, cut a piece of suitable coloured card to fit the rebates of the frame. Measure out the size of the picture in the centre of the card. If you want to make the picture appear larger in relation to the frame, make this area larger than the picture itself, but remember that the original mount will then show through. Lay the card on a well protected surface and cut the centre out of the mat with a sharp Stanley knife held at an angle of 45° to give a slight bevel (diagram 8). To ensure perfect corners use a bevel guage set at an angle of 90°. Push the centre through the card so that you are left with a window through which the picture will show. Outline this window with a thin pencil line.

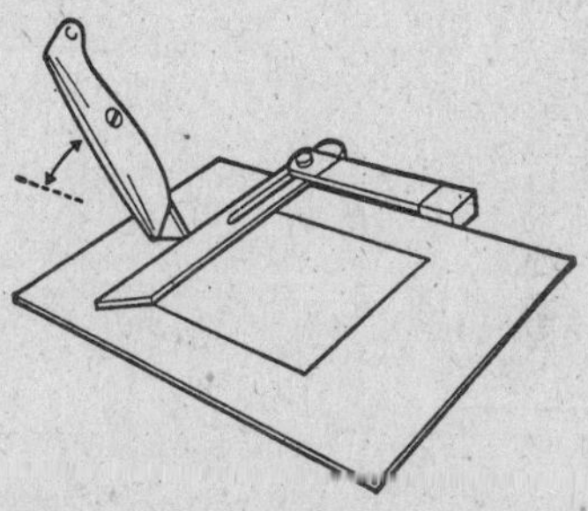

DIAGRAM 8
Cutting a window in a picture mat

f Reassemble the frame when it has been cleaned and refinished and the picture has been remounted. Turn the frame face down and slot the inner frame, if you are using one, into the rebates. Continue in the order shown in the exploded diagram 1. Make sure that the tacks holding in the backing board are secure enough to prevent the glass being loose. Do not omit the final sheet of brown paper, or dust and dirt will soon get into the frame and spoil the picture.

Cutting an over-large frame down to size (diagrams 9–11)
A frame can be fairly simply cut down to a smaller size but care must be taken to ensure that the new corners are properly mitred and fit together neatly. A basic point to remember is that it is the inner edge of the frame which must be measured to ensure that the frame will be the right size for your picture (diagram 9). Measure the length of

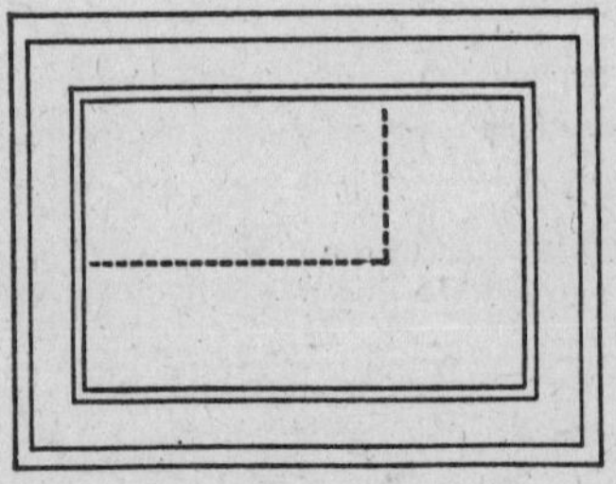

DIAGRAM 9
Measure inner edge of frame to fit picture

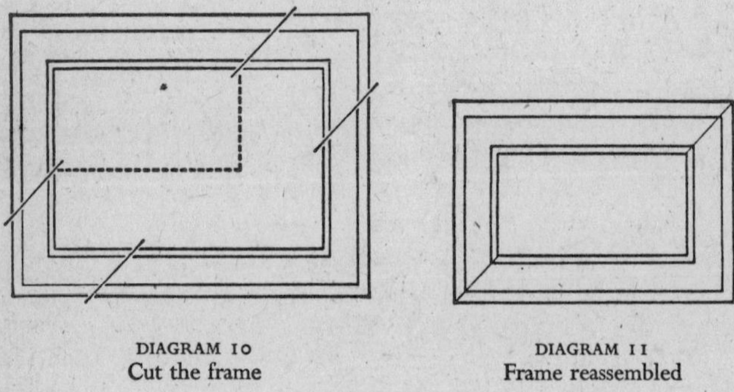

DIAGRAM 10
Cut the frame

DIAGRAM 11
Frame reassembled

frame you require from the top left-hand corner of the frame, and the depth of the frame you require from the top left-hand corner towards the bottom left-hand corner. Using a fret-saw cut the frame at these two points. Cut the wood at an angle of 45° so that the corners can be mitred. Now repeat the process, measuring the length you require along from the bottom right-hand corner and the depth required up from the bottom right-hand corner. Again make sure the wood is cut at the correct angle of 45° (diagram 10). Glue the new corners together with epoxy adhesive, making sure they are securely clamped together until the adhesive is dry. Triangular metal plates can also be used to strengthen the corners. Get a glass merchant to cut a piece of lightweight picture glass to fit the new frame.

6

Upholstery and leather

Upholstery

Upholstery can cause a lot of problems for the amateur and the usual mistake is to attempt something too ambitious before acquiring enough skill and practice to do it properly. The techniques of sprung upholstery, and the refinements such as buttoning, are simple in theory but more complex in practice. If you have not done upholstery before, begin with the simpler unsprung upholstery (this has many more possibilities than it used to have, due to the introduction of foam padding to replace springs) and progress to the more difficult methods when you have built up skill and confidence. Otherwise you run the risk of wasting money on expensive materials which can be ruined by being badly cut or pulled about. Every single re-upholstery job is slightly different. Below are typical examples of three basic types of upholstery you may want to use:

Padding directly on the frame (diagram 1)
Drop in seat (diagram 2)
Sprung seat (diagram 3)

DIAGRAM 1

DIAGRAM 2

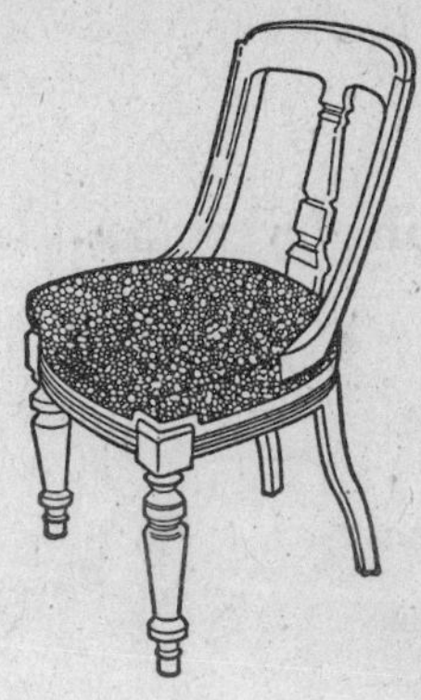

DIAGRAM 3

These should enable you to tackle most elementary upholstery. If you need more information there are many specialist books on upholstery which cover these and other upholstery techniques, such as buttoning, in very great detail.

Whichever type of upholstery you tackle, do all stripping, repairing and refinishing of the wood when the original upholstery is stripped off and before embarking on any new upholstery.

A. *Padding a box* (diagrams 4–8)

To upholster a flat-lidded box you will need a piece of high density upholstery foam about 5 cm thick, cut to the same dimensions as the lid of the box. For the cover you will need a piece of fabric the size of the lid plus the depth of the lid, plus a turning all round of about 2 cm. To cover the tacks which hold the fabric in place you will need a piece of matching braid to go round the edge of the lid.

Bevel off 3 cm of the foam 8 cm all round as shown in diagram 4.

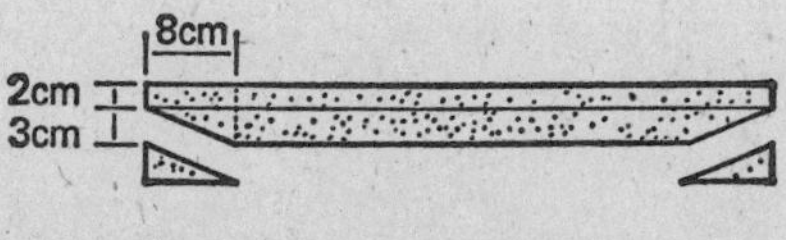

DIAGRAM 4

The excess foam can be trimmed away with scissors. (For very small or large boxes these dimensions will have to be altered to achieve the same porportions.) Stick the foam, with the smaller, bevelled side down, onto the lid of the box (diagram 5).

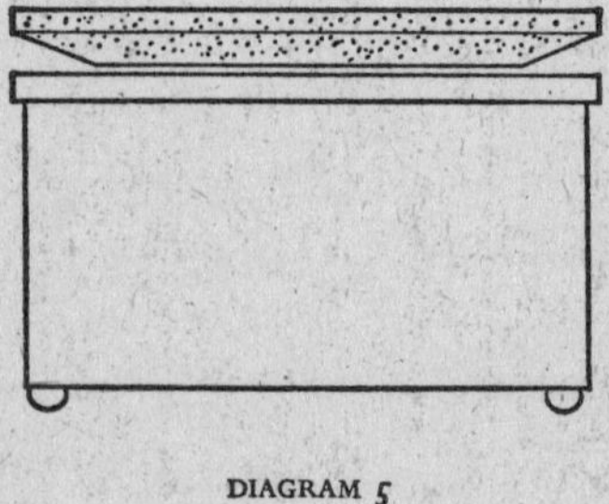

DIAGRAM 5

Lay the fabric accurately over the foam, catching it with pins in the centre to prevent it from slipping while you tack it into place. Catch the middle of each side with an upholstery tack (the standard 16 mm size—diagram 6). Do not hammer the tacks home properly until you are satisfied that the fabric lies properly. Finish tacking the front edge, working from the middle to the sides but leaving off at

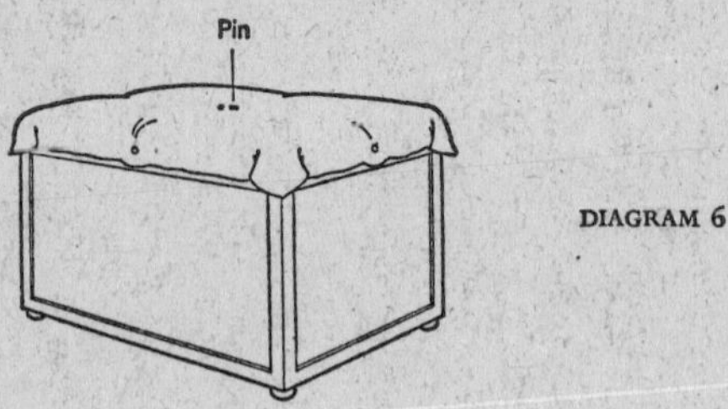

DIAGRAM 6

about 4 cm from the corners. Do the same thing to the back and then the sides, pulling the fabric into shape as you go and making sure that it is taut so that the foam is held down evenly all the way round. Finally do the corners, first tacking down the centre points then pleating the fabric neatly, cutting off the excess and tacking it down (dia-

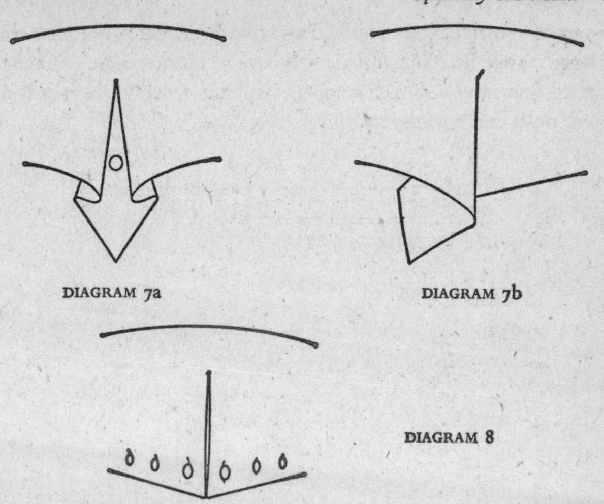

DIAGRAM 7a

DIAGRAM 7b

DIAGRAM 8

grams 7a and 7b) or more simply by squaring off the fabric and folding one side under the other (diagram 8).

Stick braid along the edges to disguise the tacks. The braid can be reinforced with gimp pins, which are very thin and can be hidden in the braid, or with brass-headed tacks which are a decorative addition

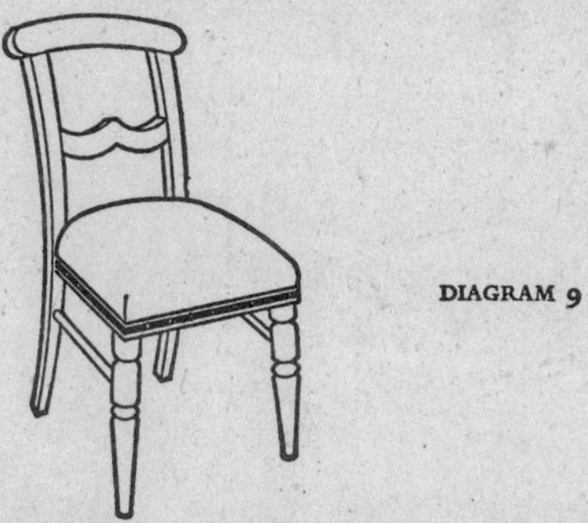

DIAGRAM 9

to the braiding as well as a reinforcement. See section *C* (diagram 26).

This very basic upholstery method can be easily adapted to make a padded seat on a chair like the one in diagram 9, where the original seating—cane, for example—is no longer serviceable. To do so you should build up a base of webbing as shown in method *B* (diagrams 10 and 11) so that the foam can rest on that instead of on the lid of the box. The webbing base should be on the upper side of the frame and filled in more densely than for standard upholstery. Use foam approximately 2½ cm deep. Calico edging 5 cm wide is stuck to the top of the foam and this, not the foam, is tacked down to the frame. (As shown in method *B*, diagrams 15 and 16) The cover is then pulled down taut over the foam and tacked around the sides of the frame.

B. Drop-in chair seat (diagrams 10–12)

First remove all the original upholstery, making a note of the order of the components. Keep the fabric cover to use as a pattern for the new cover. Use the opportunity to clean the wooden frame thoroughly and check for, and deal with, woodworm.

Replace the webbing with new webbing (old webbing will have lost its 'stretch'). Working on the upper side of the frame take the webbing first from the centre front to centre back frame. Finish working from front to back and then fix webbing from side to side, this time weaving it in and out of the front to back webbing. The method of attaching webbing strips is as follows: take the end of the roll of webbing and, with the cut edge facing into the frame, tack down with a triangle of tacks (diagram 10). Turn the webbing back on itself and fix in the same position with a further two tacks. Take

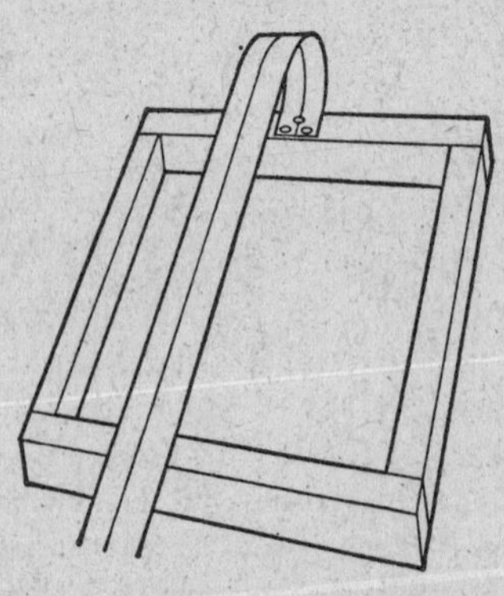

DIAGRAM 10

the webbing across the frame with a webbing stretcher. Holding the webbing taut (get someone to help you if possible) tack it down with three tacks in a triangle. Cut off the webbing with about 2½ cm to spare (diagram 11). Fold this 2½ cm back over the tacks and tack down with a further two tacks. Continue until you have built up a new base of webbing. If you know it, follow the pattern of the original webbing.

Cut a piece of hessian about 2½ cm larger all round than the drop-in frame. Use the original hessian cover as a pattern if you have it. Stretch this hessian tautly and evenly over the webbing. Tack it down about 1½ cm from the edge of the fabric. Fold the excess back over the first tacks and tack again (diagram 12).

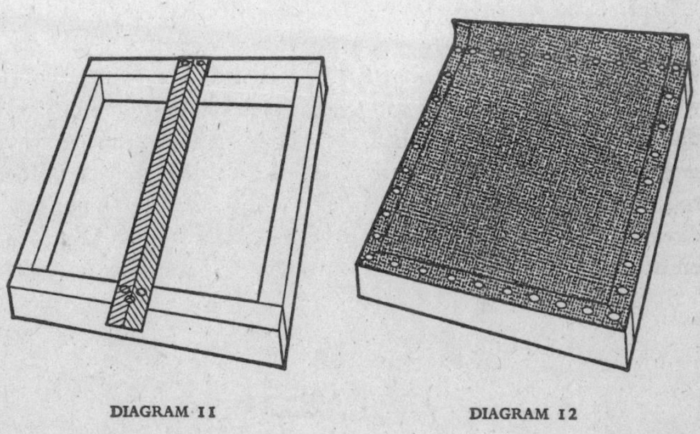

DIAGRAM 11 DIAGRAM 12

Foam

If you use foam instead of hair and wadding cut a piece of high density foam, approximately 3 cm deep, to fit the size of the drop-in frame (diagram 13). Slightly bevel the edges (diagram 14). Stick 5 cm-wide calico edging to the edges of the larger side of the foam (diagram 15).

Place the foam, small side down, onto the hessian. Tack the calico down to the frame, beginning with the centre back and front and centre sides. Finish tacking the front and back edges, working from middle to corners, and then do the sides. The foam should form an

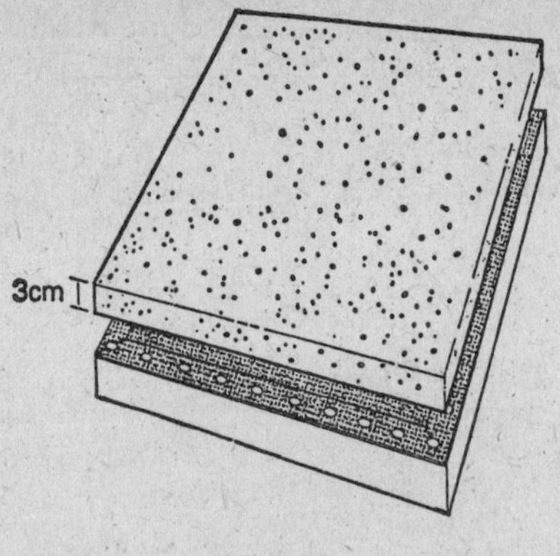

DIAGRAM 13

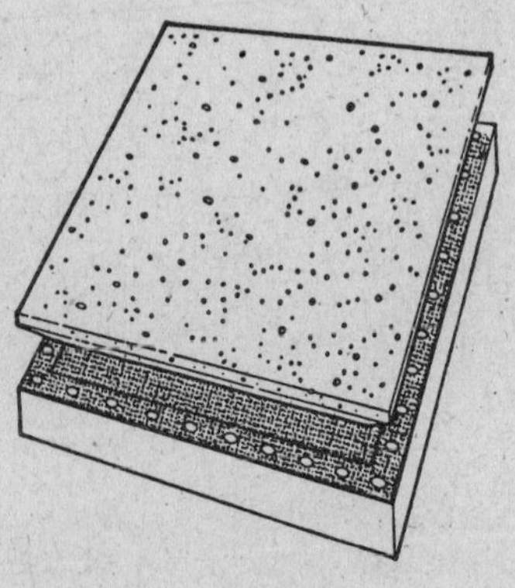

DIAGRAM 14

even dome (diagram 16). Do not drive the tacks in fully until you are satisfied that the foam is in the correct shape.

Fix the cover over the foam, turning it in and tacking it *under* the frame. At the corners tack down the centre point and fold in the material neatly, tacking it in place. Cut away any excess material to avoid lumpiness (diagram 17).

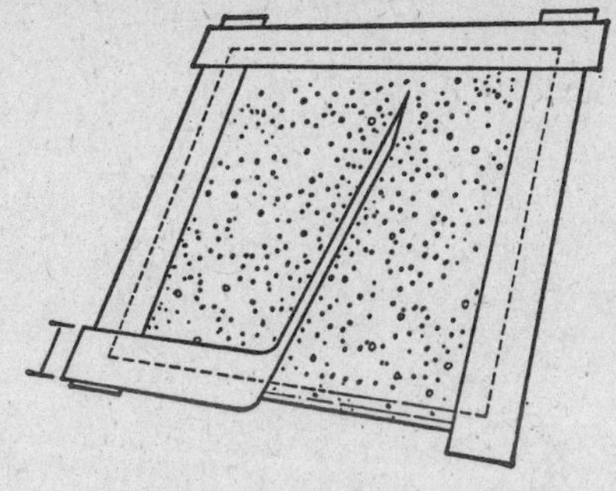

DIAGRAM 15

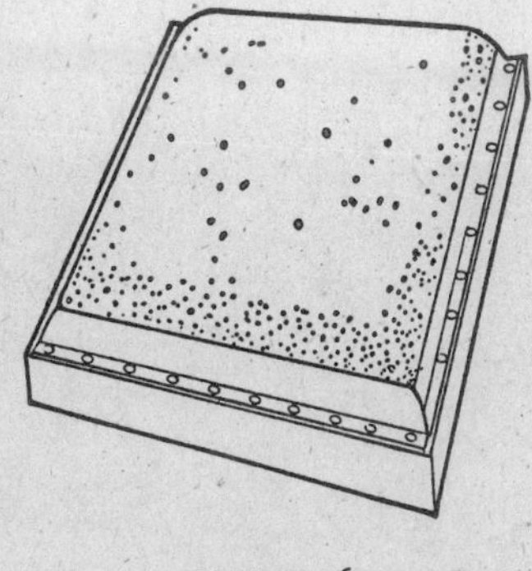

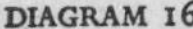

DIAGRAM 16

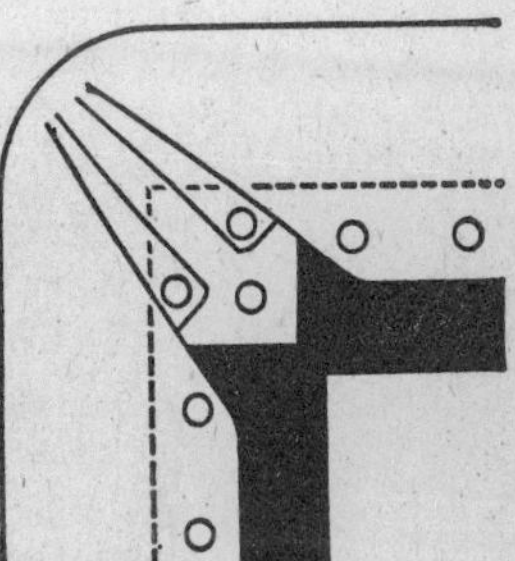

DIAGRAM 17

Traditional hair and wadding stuffing

Old hair stuffing can be re-used if it is cleaned and aired, but new stuffing makes the work easier. Keep the calico and top covers to use as patterns for their replacements. Cover the hessian with loops of twine about 15 cm long (diagram 18). These loops are used to anchor the hair in position. The hair is placed under the loops and teased out to cover the hessian and make an even stuffing of about 2½ cm in depth (diagram 19). Cover the hair with a piece of calico, stretched taut and tacked down under the frame. Do not drive the tacks in fully until you are sure the seat is a symmetrical shape. Fold in the calico at the corners and cut away excess material to avoid lumpiness.

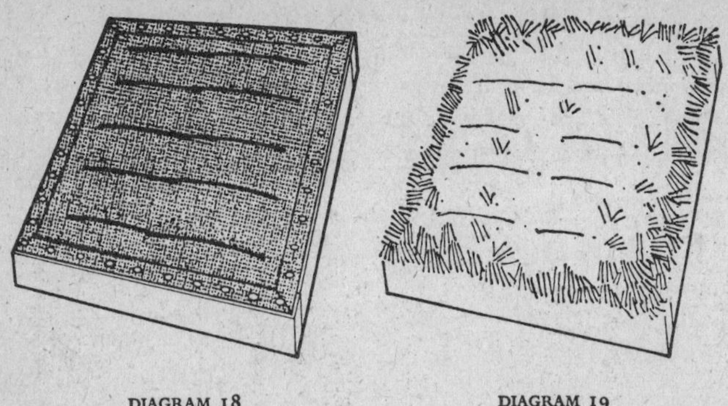

DIAGRAM 18 DIAGRAM 19

Now lay the wadding over the calico cover, again making sure the seat is properly shaped (diagram 20). The top cover is placed over the wadding, correctly centred (this is particularly important if you are working with patterned material) and turned in and tacked down under the frame, as described for foam stuffing (diagram 17).

Whichever method you use, the underside of the seat should be covered with a piece of hessian or similar strong fabric. This is turned in and tacked onto the frame (diagram 21).

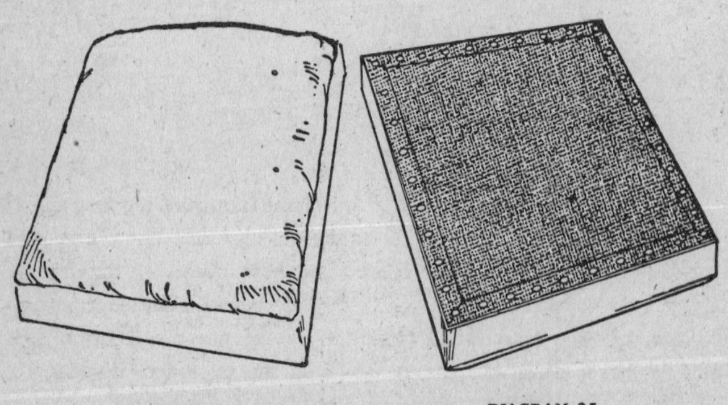

DIAGRAM 20 DIAGRAM 21

C. *Sprung upholstery—dining chair* (*Advanced*) (diagrams 22–27)

a Take the original upholstery off the chair, making a note of the components and the order in which you took them off the frame. A ripping chisel and a mallet are the best tools for this job but you can improvise with an old screwdriver or something similar. Take care not to damage any materials you might like to use again. Also take care not to damage the wood. While the frame is bare do any necessary repairs and refinishing. Treat for woodworm.

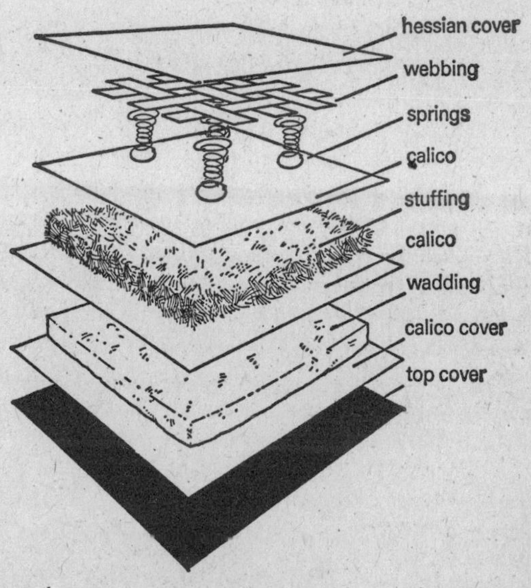

DIAGRAM 22

The more complex the piece of furniture the more important it is to make an accurate note of the sequence of layers. Where arms and back are upholstered as well as the seat, techniques vary slightly and you should copy accurately what was done before. On a sprung upholstered dining chair the sequence will, with the possibility of one or two minor variations, be as shown in the exploded diagram 22. That is:—

A hessian cover—to neaten the work and keep out dust;

Webbing—usually flax webbing in an old chair. A modern chair may have rubber webbing. Flax webbing cannot be restretched and will have to be replaced. Rubber webbing may be re-usable. The webbing is fixed *under* the frame;

Springs—sewn to the webbing where the strips cross. If the springs are undamaged they can be re-used on fresh webbing. If you replace one spring you should replace them all, as the new one will have more 'spring' than the others and will upset the balance of the seat;

A calico or hessian cover—sewn over the springs and tacked down to the chair frame. Keep this as a pattern for a new one;

Stuffing—usually horse hair or kapok. It can usually be re-used if aired thoroughly and fluffed up. Check for clothes moth etc.;

Calico-cover—tacked down, to keep stuffing in place;

Wadding—a layer of very soft stuffing which gives the seat a good shape;

A calico cover—over the wadding;

Top cover—keep this as a pattern for the new cover. When choosing a fabric for the new cover bear in mind the type of wear it will get as well as its appearance. Until you are fairly skilled at stretching and tacking down the cover avoid striped patterns which draw attention to every imperfection and avoid velvets because you may not be able to get the nap to lie straight.

b Turn the chair upside down and attach the webbing to the underside of the frame. Follow the technique described in section *B* (diagram 10). The tighter you stretch the webbing the firmer the seat will be.

c Turn the chair the right way up and sew the springs to the webbing at the point where it interlaces. For best results use strong upholsterer's twine and a curved upholsterer's needle. Use the stitch shown in diagram 23. Five springs is the average number for this type of chair—one set in the middle and four in a square round it. However you should copy the original pattern wherever possible. These springs are then compressed to a height of approximately 35 cm by tying cord to the top of them and tying or tacking the other end of the cord to the frame (diagram 24).

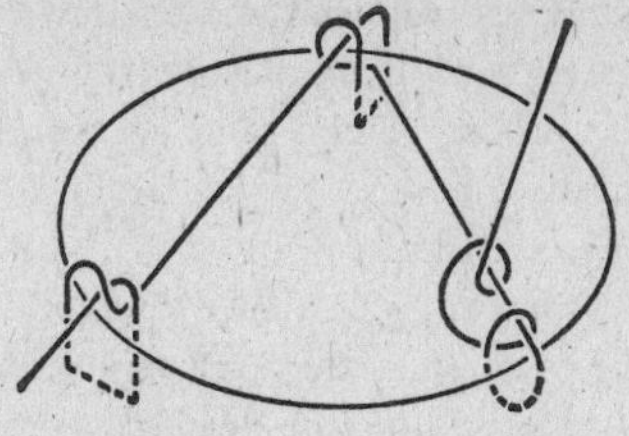

DIAGRAM 23

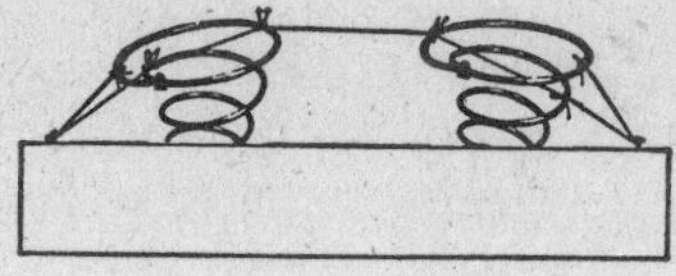

DIAGRAM 24

d Cover the springs with a hessian or calico cover. Use the original to make a pattern. The tops of the springs are then sewn to this cover with twine, using the special knot (diagram 23). Use four knots for each spring and make sure the springs are perfectly upright.

e Cover the hessian with loops of twine about 15 cm apart as in section *B* (diagram 18). Arrange the kapok or horsehair stuffing on the hessian, teasing it through the loops to keep it anchored down and in a good shape. Make sure it overlaps the hard edges of the chair. At this stage the uncompressed stuffing should be about 11 cm deep.

f Cover the stuffing with a calico cover, cut using the original as a pattern. The calico must be eased into shape and tacked to the frame using the method described in section *A* (diagram 6), for fixing the cover over the foam stuffing. It should control the stuffing to the correct shape and compress it down to a depth of about 4 cm.

g Arrange a layer of wadding on the calico, securing it with a few loops of twine (diagram 25).

h Tack a calico cover over the wadding.

i The final cover can now be put on. This should be cut out using the original cover as a pattern. Tack this cover to the frame in the manner already described in section *A* (diagram 6), that is, securing

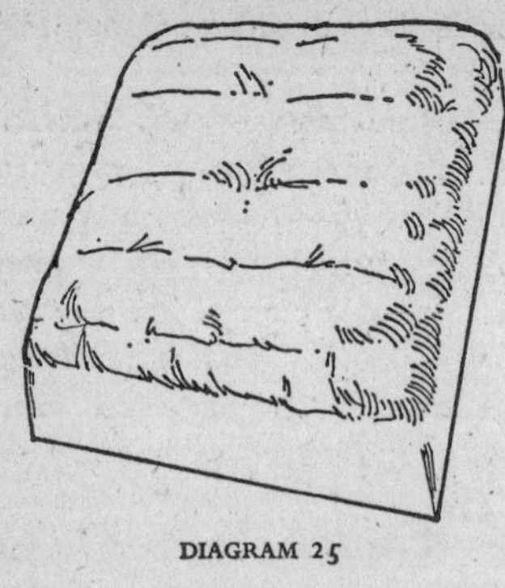

DIAGRAM 25

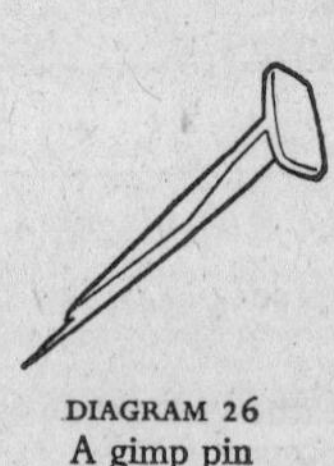

DIAGRAM 26
A gimp pin

the front and back and working towards the corners, then securing the sides. Do not drive in the tacks until you are satisfied with the appearance of the seat.

j Cover all the tacks with decorative braid—you can buy very wide braid if you have a lot of mistakes to disguise. This braid can be glued down and/or tacked to the frame with brass-headed upholstery pins or gimp pins which can be hidden under the braid (diagram 26).

k Turn the chair upside down and finish off with a cover of hessian or black linen tacked underneath the frame (diagram 21).

Foam

The metal springs and horsehair or kapok stuffing (stages *c–e*) can be replaced with high density upholstery foam. This simplifies the whole process although the end result will not be quite as comfortable and springy as a traditionally upholstered chair.

Cut a cube of foam to fit snugly inside the frame on the webbing base. It should lie a little higher than the top of the frame to allow for compression. Continue from stage *f* making sure the calico controls the foam to the correct shape.

Leather

Cleaning

Leather looks robust but is usually very thin, especially when used for book binding and desk tops. Care should be taken while cleaning, as over zealous rubbing may tear the leather. Always avoid the gilding when cleaning as this is easily rubbed off.

Grease marks are best treated with an absorbent such as fuller's earth or talcum powder. Sprinkle the powder onto the mark and brush it off when it has absorbed the grease. Really stubborn stains on fairly robust leather, such as a hide-covered chair, can be gently rubbed with a little of one of the proprietary grease solvents containing a substance such as carbon tetrachloride. An alternative is to wipe the leather with a linen pad wrung out in methylated spirit. Never soak leather with any of these solvents as this will create a new stain.

Leather which is simply grubby can be carefully wiped with a cloth wrung out in warm, soapy water and then 'rinsed' by wiping with a clean cloth wrung out in fresh warm water. Pat dry, and polish when thoroughly dry with a good quality leather polish. Leather which has become very grimy should be cleaned with Saddle Soap used according to the maker's instructions.

Preserving and renovating

Leather will stay supple and last longer if it is given frequent but light applications of a good quality leather polish or cream such as 'Hide Food'. These preparations clean the leather as they polish it. Delicate leather, like the paper-thin leather used for book bindings, can be conditioned with a sparing application of warmed lanolin to keep it supple, and then polished after a few hours when the lanolin has had time to soak in. Pale leathers can be kept supple with a very sparing application of petroleum jelly worked well into the leather.

There are a number of colouring paints and polishes available for restoring colour to leather which has faded or been damaged in some way. You may find them in art or craft shops. However they can be quite easily obtained from less immediately obvious sources such as shoe repair shops. Another type of leather colour with a wider application than the one for which it is sold is the renovating paint for use on car upholstery. When using any of these colourants make certain you know whether or not they are meant to change the colour of the leather permanently or whether they can be cleaned off.

Tears—on furniture

Leather for making patches for hide-covered furniture, and other useful items like needles intended especially for leather work, can usually be bought from craft shops. They are primarily intended for making new articles such as leather belts and bags but are extremely useful when small quantities of leather and special tools are required for repairs.

Small tears can be patched over directly. Long tears should be sewn together before patching to restore enough tension to the base leather for the patch to stick properly (diagram 1). Cut a patch to cover the damaged area, making sure it is a little larger than strictly necessary from the cosmetic point of view. It is very important for the patch to be large enough to stick firmly to the original leather. Chamfer the edges (diagram 2) by scraping with a sharp cutting tool such as a Stanley knife, so that the patch eventually fits as flush as possible with

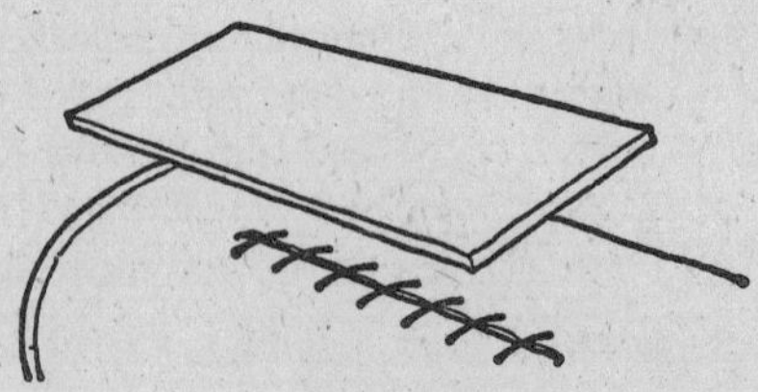

DIAGRAM 1
Sew tears before patching over

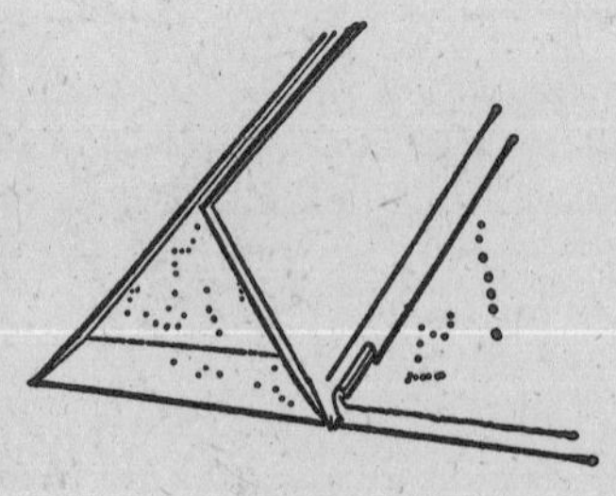

DIAGRAM 2
Scrape edges of patch so that the repair does not stand proud

the underlying leather. Wipe over the patch and the area to which it is being stuck with methylated spirit. This will remove traces of grease and allow the adhesive to work as efficiently as possible. Almost any adhesive will stick leather to leather but an epoxy adhesive gives the most secure repair. If the tear is very large do not use an epoxy adhesive as it makes a very stiff patch, without any flexibility, which is liable to crack if stretched.

Tears—on book bindings

To patch book bindings you need extremely thin leather available from specialist suppliers which you should be able to find through the yellow pages or classified advertisements of the telephone directory.

Tidy up the damaged area with a pair of sharp scissors so that the patch to be replaced is a manageable shape such as a square (diagram 3). Trace this shape onto tracing paper and then use the tracing to cut out an identical patch in fresh leather. When cutting out the patch make it fractionally larger all round than the original (diagram 4). Wipe over the leather and the patch with methylated spirit to remove all traces of grease. Apply a thin layer of adhesive to the wrong side of the leather patch. Place it in position, tucking the edges underneath the old leather and sticking the edges of the old leather down

DIAGRAM 3
Tidy up damaged area into a regular shape

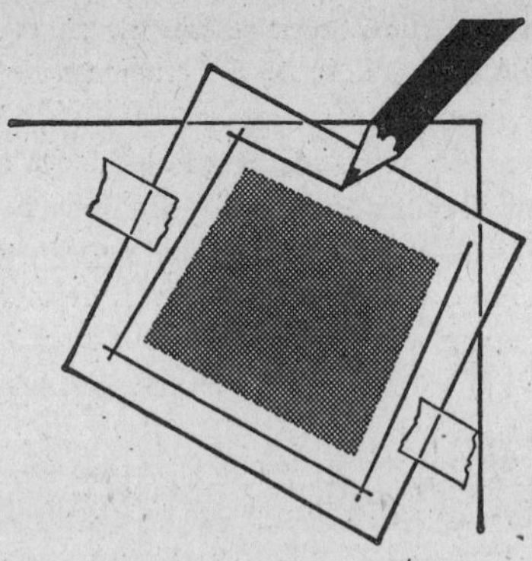

DIAGRAM 4
Trace and cut a patch slightly larger than the damaged area

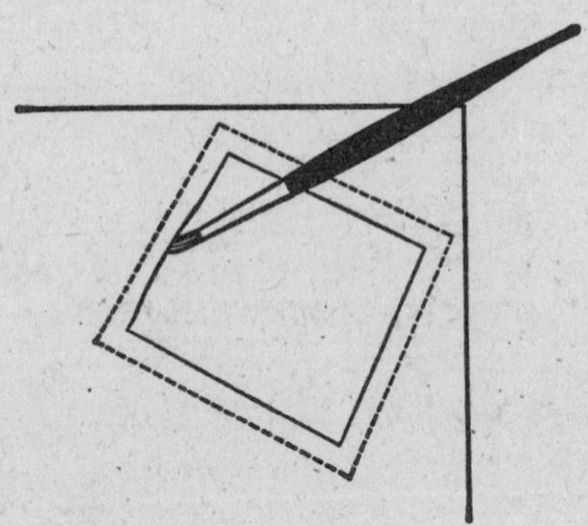

DIAGRAM 5
Apply adhesive to underside of original leather

onto the new patch by applying a little adhesive with a thin brush to the underside of the original leather (diagram 5). Wipe away all excess adhesive. Weight the repair and leave to dry.

Relining leather-topped desks (*Advanced*)
If a leather desk top is sufficiently badly damaged to warrant replacement, scrape away any remnants of the original and use a solvent and an abrasive paper to remove all traces of glue. You will find that the

leather lies in a very shallow recess so that the top of the leather lies flush with the top of the desk. New leather can be obtained from craft shops.

Measure out the area to be recovered on a piece of brown paper and cut a template. Try the template for size to make sure it is accurate before you use it as a pattern for cutting the leather. It is unlikely that the area to be recovered will be a perfectly symmetrical shape. Using a sharp Stanley knife, cut the leather a fraction larger all round than the template to allow minor adjustments and possible shrinkage when the glue is applied.

Apply the adhesive with a brush for speed, being careful not to let the leather get too wet. Place the leather in position without pulling and stretching it. Press out any air bubbles. When the glue is almost dry, cut off any excess leather with a Stanley knife and press down

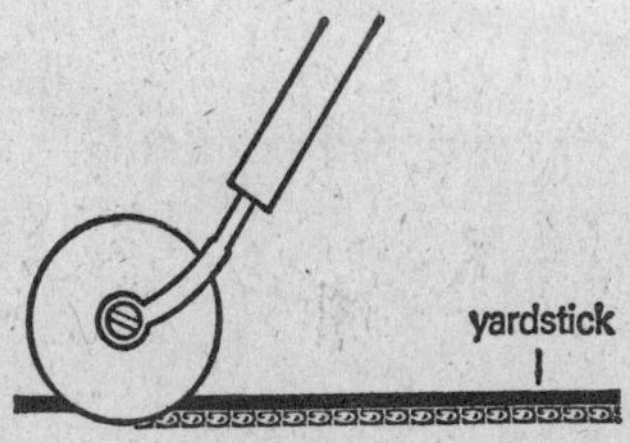

DIAGRAM 6
Keep tooling wheel straight with a yardstick

the edges. Make sure all excess glue is wiped away and weight the leather down, paying particular attention to the corners, until the glue has dried thoroughly.

The traditional patterns frequently found round the edges of the leather are made with a special tooling wheel. These are available at some art shops. The wheel is heated (take care not to over-heat) and then drawn around the edge of the leather using a yardstick as a guide (diagram 6).

Gilding

Leather is often gilded. The tooled pattern around the edge of leather desk tops is usually done over a transfer tape of gold foil. As the hot

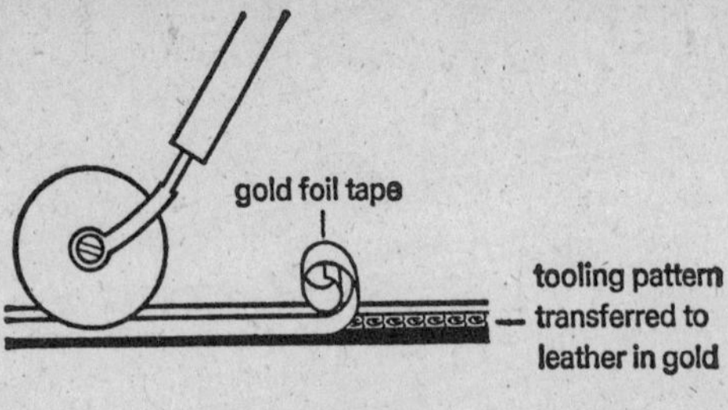

DIAGRAM 7

wheel is drawn over the tape the pattern is transferred to the leather in gold (diagram 7).

If you have artistic flair the same gold transfer tape can be used to tidy up or replace missing gilt lettering on leather book bindings. Freehand lettering or patterns drawn directly on to the back of the tape will be transferred direct to the leather. Alternatively you can use gold transfer foil which is printed on to the leather by being rubbed gently on the back with a sharp pencil.

7

Bamboo, cane and rush

Bamboo

'Bamboo' is a term used for many different types of grasses and palms as well as for furniture made from the giant bamboo grass itself. Most furniture of this type is held together by binding with thin canes rather than by conventional woodworking methods. This makes it difficult to mend and awkward to clean.

Cleaning

Bamboo furniture rarely gets dirty enough to warrant harsh cleaning methods. Frequent dusting and an occasional wipe with a damp cloth should be all that is required. Natural bamboo looks better if it is given a polish with a good quality wax polish, and this helps to protect it. A wax polish usually revitalises an old piece of bamboo furniture. Clean off layers of old polish with methylated spirit and start afresh with a good quality wax polish.

Bamboo which has been badly neglected needs a thorough wash with a mild detergent solution. Use a wide paint-brush or a scrubbing brush if the dirt is ingrained. Make sure all the detergent is rinsed off afterwards.

Mending

Since most bamboo furniture is made by bending it into shape and binding, the usual problem will be that the binding has given way, threatening imminent collapse. Rebind with split cane or a synthetic substitute such as plastic. Synthetics can only be used if you are going to paint the furniture afterwards. The same drying-out process which has caused the disintegration of the binding will also have affected the bamboo and you will find it very brittle and almost impossible to bend back into the required shape. Deal with this problem by soaking the bamboo in very hot water to soften it up. You will find it easier to work if someone helps you hold the bamboo in position while it is being bound.

The thicker, real bamboo, may be solid enough to allow more conventional woodworking repairs with nails and screws. Remember, however, that the canes will be hollow and that repairs of this kind will be much more difficult. Depending on the type of repair required you can try filling the hollow with a filler such as Interior Polyfilla to give a better base. Drill when the filler is dry and use a conventional masonry plug to give the screw a good grip. You need great care while drilling bamboo as it tends to split along the direction of its fibres. Use the correct wood auger with the drill and work slowly. Obviously you will not want to countersink the screws as this will weaken their grip still further. The tops of small screws which lie on the surface can be simply camouflaged with a little paint or lacquer.

Where the bamboo is supporting weight and looks as though it might be splintering you can strengthen it by inserting a piece of dowelling (see p. 13ff). Although the bamboo pole is basically hollow you will need to drill carefully through the blockage which occurs at each ring. If the bit on your drill is not long enough to reach the full length of the bamboo the blockages can be carefully burned through with a red hot steel rod. Tidy up splintery fragments by sticking them down on the dowel with woodworkers' adhesive.

Finishing

Natural bamboo is given a wax finish with good quality wax polish. Alternative finishes are clear polyurethane and paint. Whenever possible a spray finish will achieve the best results. Use several thin coats, allowing each coat to dry before applying the next one.

Caring for cane and wicker

The fibres of wicker and cane furniture will eventually give way and need replacing, but you can do a lot to retard this by making sure that furniture is not allowed to dry out unnecessarily. A centrally heated atmosphere is especially harmful. A humidifier, particularly an efficient electric one, will greatly benefit cane and wicker as well as the rest of your furniture. In addition it is a good idea to wipe cane over once a month with a damp sponge. This will also help to keep it clean. Wicker can be hosed down once a year or so, or covered with sheets of wet paper. Do not use cane and wicker furniture before it has dried out thoroughly as this will stretch the fibres and weaken them.

Cleaning

Natural and painted wicker should be wiped down with a damp cloth. The colour of natural wicker can be preserved and enhanced by washing with a weak solution of hydrogen peroxide (9 litres water to 225 ml hydrogen peroxide). The addition of a little vinegar to the solution is good for the golden colour of the wicker.

Really dirty cane can be 'washed' with a cloth wrung out in warm soapy water and then rinsed several times with cloths wrung out in clear water. Soap left on cane will encourage mould.

Finishing

Wicker can be painted or varnished. A spray paint is best for getting into nooks and crannies. Several thin coats are infinitely better than one thick coat. Cane will look naturally shiny but a coat of clear varnish is a good idea to give protection against dirt and damp.

Whiskery fibres should be sanded off before painting or varnishing. Use the finest grade glasspaper.

Caning chairs (Advanced)

Chairs in need of recaning either have to be cleared of old broken cane to leave a clean frame, or frequently a hardboard or canvas seat, which has been nailed over the broken original seating, has to be removed. You will find a nail punch and hammer useful for clearing cane which has been wedged firmly into the holes. At this stage do any other repairs and cleaning which you consider necessary (see p. 8) and give fresh glue and surfaces time to dry thoroughly before starting to recane.

Measure the diameter of the holes of the grid in order to determine the size of cane you will require. For the standard six-strand pattern dealt with here (diagram 9) you will find that at least four strands of cane will need to go through each hole and probably extra cane will be needed to neaten and protect the border. Cane comes in standard, numbered sizes and it is best to get a list of those available from your supplier and plan exactly the quantity and size you will need for the job before you start. You can juggle the sizes to fit the hole size and to add interest to the weave, but always use a medium cane to give strength to the basic mesh and keep the finer cane for the decorative interweaving: 75g cane will be sufficient for an average chair seat.

The tools needed for hand caning can easily be improvised. You will need half a dozen pegs for wedging cane into holes, but if you have nothing you can adapt, these can be made by sharpening pieces of dowelling. Small, stubby pencils usually work well. You will also need a large headed needle for threading the strands of cane through the weave—something suitable can be bought from an upholsterer's supplier. Another useful tool is a long needle to hold down the strands already woven in the correct pattern while you thread fresh cane through. A knitting needle is often suitable.

Your hands may get sore pulling on the damp cane, so wear a pair of flexible gloves.

Method

Place the canes to soak in warm water so that they become pliable enough to weave. They will then dry out on the frame and remain firmly in place. Dampen cane you are currently working on with a damp sponge. The cane will thread more easily if you sharpen the ends first.

1. Diagram 1. If you are working on a totally rectangular frame start from a corner and work vertically across the frame. Draw the cane up through the first hole leaving 5 cm hanging down and jam the cane with a peg. Bring the rest of the cane across to the equivalent hole on the opposite side of the frame and thread it down, bringing it up through the adjacent hole and back to the opposite hole on the original side. Make sure the shiny surface of the cane is uppermost. Continue until you have finished working vertically.

2. Diagram 2. Repeat the process horizontally over the first layer, using the other two sides of the frame, to make a basic mesh.

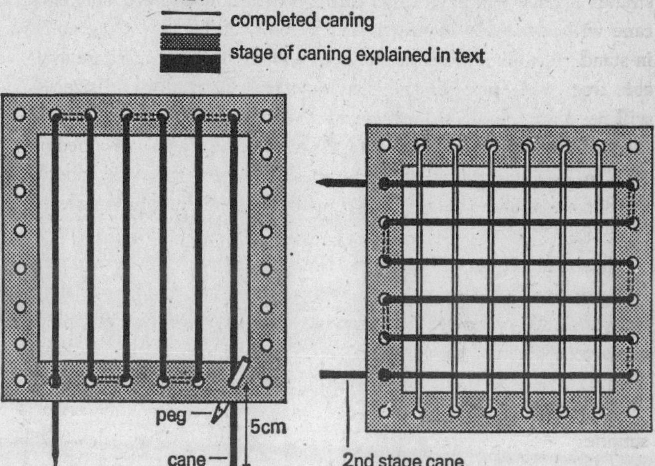

DIAGRAM I
First vertical strand

DIAGRAM 2
First horizontal strand

3a. Diagram 3a. After the first three or four strands have been woven and jammed into their holes, wrap the end of the cane, which you left hanging down, round the adjacent loop. When it dries it will shrink slightly to make a secure join. *Fasten off* in exactly the same way, cutting off excess cane and leaving just enough for a secure join. Use the same method to *add on fresh strands of cane.*

3b. Diagram 3b. Alternatively, wrap the sharpened end of the old cane round the beginning of the new cane for approximately 2

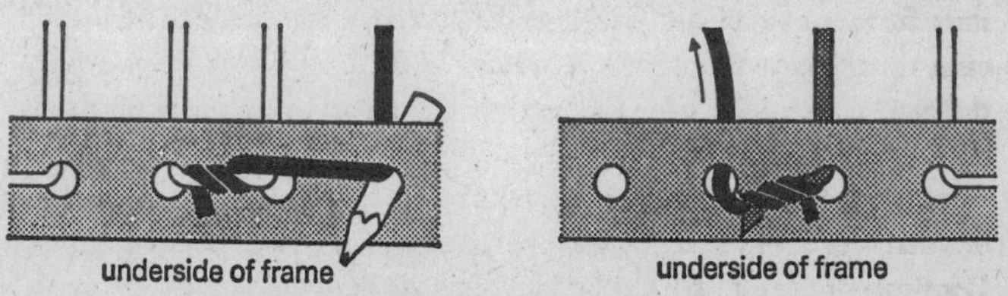

DIAGRAM 3a and 3b
Fastening off, tidying loose strands and adding fresh strands

cm, as if you were wrapping two strands of knitting wool together. When you continue with the new strand, pulling it tautly through the next hole and wedging it securely, the two ends will dry round each other to make a firm join. All joins should be made so that they lie *underneath* the frame and out of sight. You may well find that you need to redamp the canes with a wet sponge as you work, particularly when twisting to make a join.

4. Diagram 4. When working with a shape which is not a rectangle the principle is exactly the same, except that you start from the centre of the frame and work outwards in order to make sure that you start using the sides of the frame at the right stage. To do this on

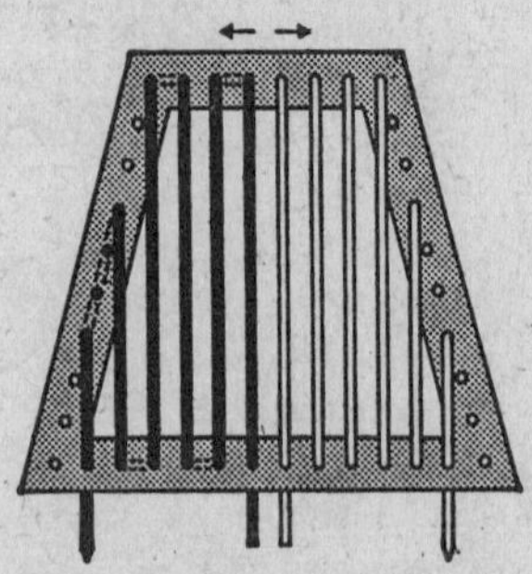

DIAGRAM 4
Keeping strands parallel on a non-rectangular frame

a small job where one strand of cane will be sufficient for the first stage of the mesh, mark the middle of the cane. Draw it up through the centre hole and jam it at this half-way mark, so that there is an equal amount of cane for each side of the frame. Proceed in the usual way, taking care when you run out of holes on the opposite side of the frame that you carry the cane to the correct hole in the side of the frame to form a perfectly parallel weave. On a large area start with a fresh strand of cane for each half of the frame.

5a. Diagram 5a. The basic horizontal and vertical mesh must now be repeated, unless the caning is for a part of the furniture which takes no strain, in which case it can sometimes be omitted. This second layer should never be omitted on chair seats. Repeat the first

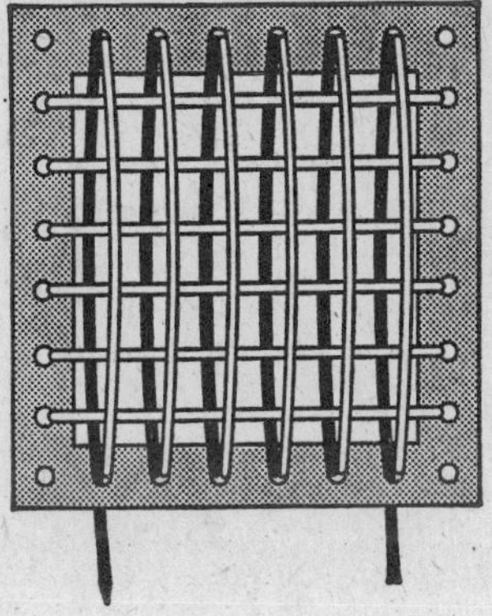

DIAGRAM 5a
Second vertical strand

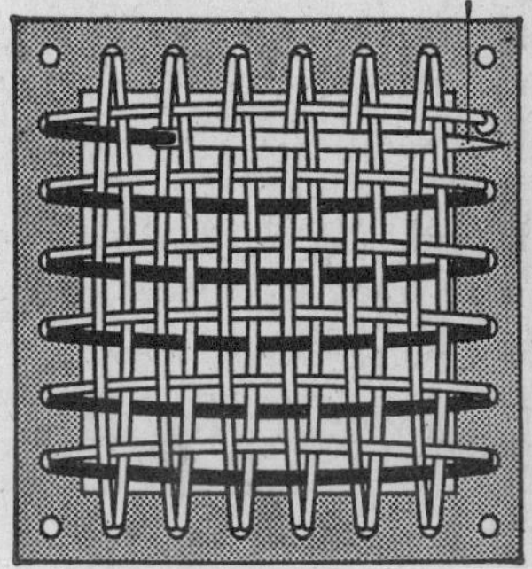

DIAGRAM 5b
Second horizontal strand

stage exactly, so that there is a vertical layer of cane on either side of the horizontal strands.

5b. Diagram 5b. Repeat the second stage, but this time the second set of horizontal strands must weave under and over the two vertical strands of cane. This is where the guiding tool will begin to come into its own, picking out the pattern so that the cane can be easily slipped through the mesh.

6. Diagram 6. The next stage is the *diagonal weaving*. Separate all four strands of cane, making sure they are clearly in their pairs. Use the guiding tool for this. At this point it is best to thread the cane using a needle and to pick out the pattern in advance with a guiding tool.

Starting at the lower right-hand corner, take the cane *under the vertical* pairs and *over the horizontal* pairs to arrive at the top left-hand corner. When you have worked one half of the frame in this direction start again at the lower right-hand corner and work in exactly the same direction over the other side of the chair.

To get the diagonals sloping the opposite way and to complete the six-strand pattern, start from the lower left-hand corner and work towards the top right-hand corner taking the cane *under the horizontal* pairs and *over* the vertical pairs.

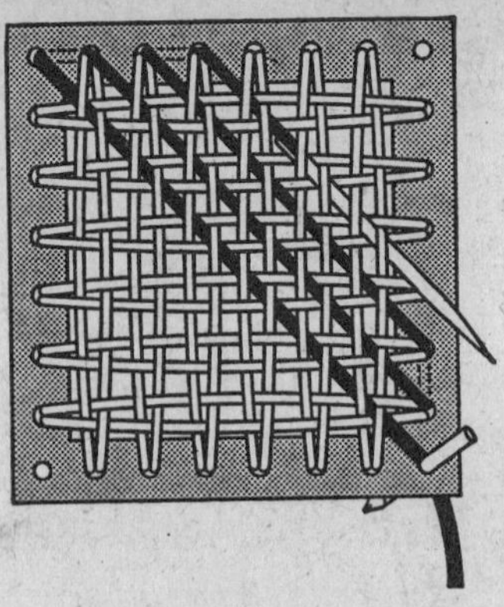

DIAGRAM 6
Diagonal Weaving

7. Diagrams 7a and b, 8. Neaten the caning and protect it by giving it an edging of wider cane. This will also help the cane to remain secure in the holes when it dries and shrinks. Cut one length of wider cane for each side, leaving each length 5 cm longer than the side of the frame it is to cover. Sharpen the ends of the cane as usual. Push the end of each edging cane into the end holes on the appropriate side of the frame, leaving 2 cm at each end for fastening. Secure with pegs. Be sure to keep the shiny side uppermost.

The edging cane should then be secured with a much finer cane brought up and down into each hole along the full length of the side of the chair you are edging—looping over the edging cane each time. Begin in the hole adjacent to the corner hole. If the holes are already very jammed with canes you may need to take this securing cane into

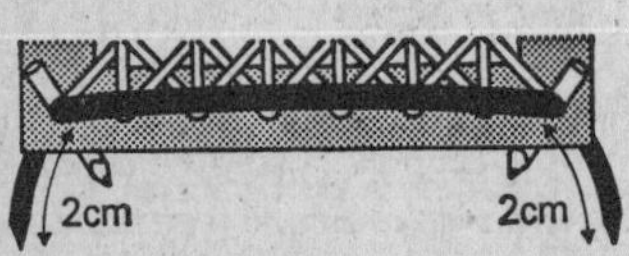

DIAGRAM 7a

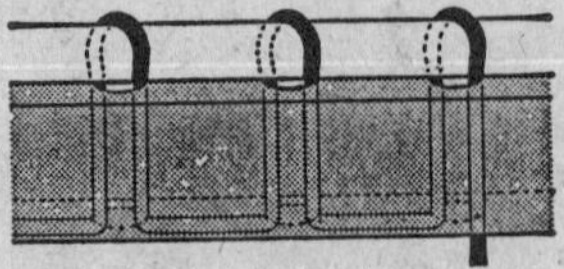

DIAGRAM 7b

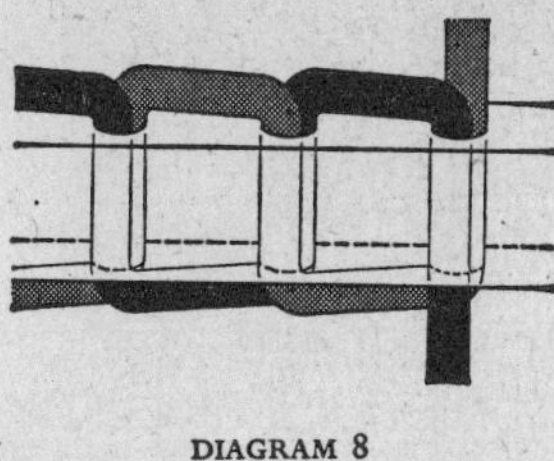

DIAGRAM 8

alternate holes. Secure and neaten all the ends as in 3. An alternative method of edging is simply to take a thick cane (grade 5 or 6) round the frame twice from hole to hole.

DIAGRAM 9

8. As long as the cane has been worked throughout with the shiny side uppermost it is not essential to do anything further. However you may prefer to give an extra finish such as a clear varnish when the cane has really dried out. A spray finish is easiest to use.

Using pre-woven cane

Pre-woven cane is often used on reproduction furniture or it may be used to repair furniture originally caned by hand. It should be cared for in the same way as conventional cane and is quite simple to replace.

Pre-woven cane webbing is usually available through suppliers of upholstery materials.

Method

Remove all traces of the original cane and spline with a mallet and small chisel; clean out the groove into which it was glued. All the old glue should be thoroughly wiped away using an appropriate solvent (p. 147). Make a card template of the area to be recovered and use this as a guide to cutting out an accurate shape in the fresh webbing. Cut the cane so that it extends about 2 cm beyond the groove into which it fits (diagram 1). Make sure it is cut in such a way that the weave is not crooked.

Soak the webbing in hot water until pliable. Position it over the chair-frame, shiny side uppermost, and work the webbing firmly into

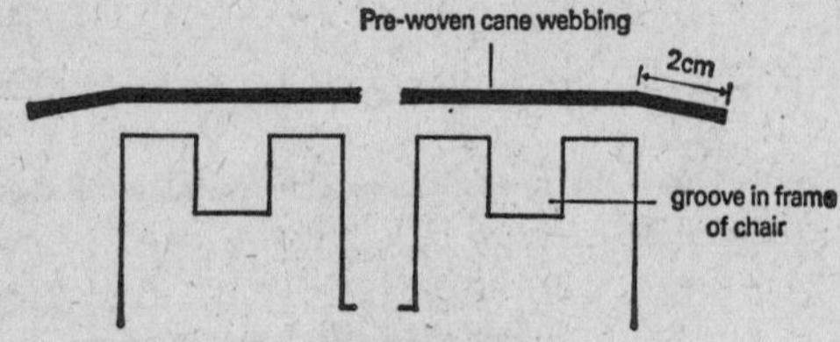

DIAGRAM 1
Place webbing over frame, allow 2 cms all round

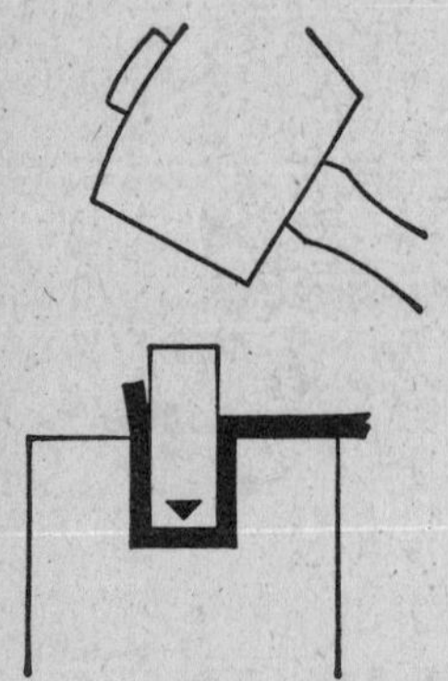

DIAGRAM 2
Work dampened cane into groove with a mallet and peg

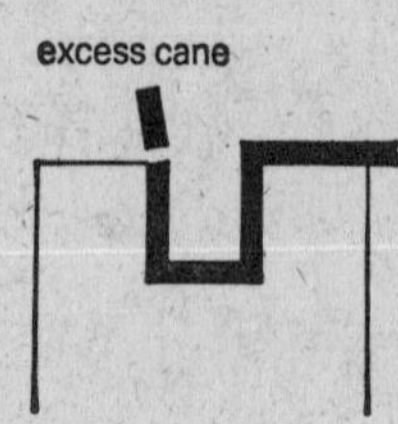

DIAGRAM 3
Trim off excess cane

the groove with a mallet and peg (diagram 2). Work the front and back sides of the frame first as this will make it easier to achieve the right tension. The webbing will become tauter when it dries and will dry into the shape of the groove.

Trim off the excess webbing with a sharp razor just below the edge of the groove (diagram 3).

The webbing is kept in place by a flexible strip of wood (spline) the same depth as the groove, glued into the groove over the cane. Use a woodworking glue to fix the spline into position. Squeeze this glue fairly liberally into the groove over the cane. Soak the wooden strip in hot water until pliable and wipe off the excess moisture. Position it in the groove and fix it with a mallet and peg (diagram 4). Position the wooden strip so that the ends meet in the least conspicuous place.

On a rectangular frame use four strips and mitre the corners (diagram 5) for a good fit.

Wipe off excess glue before it dries. The wood strip should fit flush with the edge of the frame.

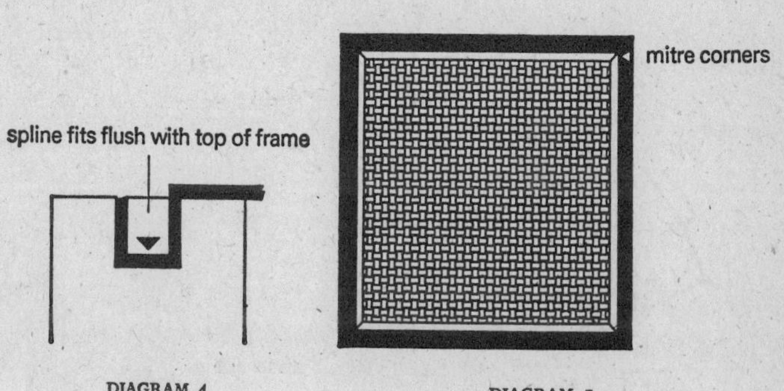

DIAGRAM 4
Flexible spline holds cane in position

DIAGRAM 5
On a square frame mitre corners of spline

Rush weaving

Natural rush seats can be replaced with a little care and patience. These days few people use natural straw which is difficult to keep at a uniform thickness and which has to be constantly spliced together to make a continuous length. Paper fibre is now frequently used as a substitute. This is available from most craft shops. However you can use the rush weave pattern with any natural or synthetic fibre you like, as long as it is strong enough. A ball of fibre weighing 1½ kilos will be more than adequate for an average dining chair.

Method

This is the method for renewing rush seats in the traditional four-triangle pattern (diagram A), using a synthetic fibre.

1 Tack the end of the cord underneath the frame at the top right-hand side then fasten it securely by knotting round the frame;
2 Bring the cord across the frame, over and under the front rail of the frame;
3 Pass the cord over and under the right rail of the chair;
4 Take the cord across the frame and over and under the left-hand rail;
5 Pass the cord over and under the front rail of the chair;
6 Take the cord across the frame and over and under the back rail;
7 Pass the cord over and under the left-hand rail;
8 Take the cord across the frame and over and under the right-hand rail;
9 Pass the cord over and under the back rail.

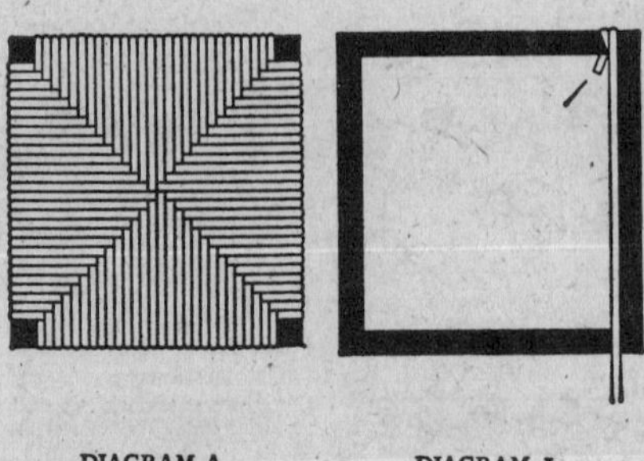

DIAGRAM A
Four-triangle pattern

DIAGRAM 1

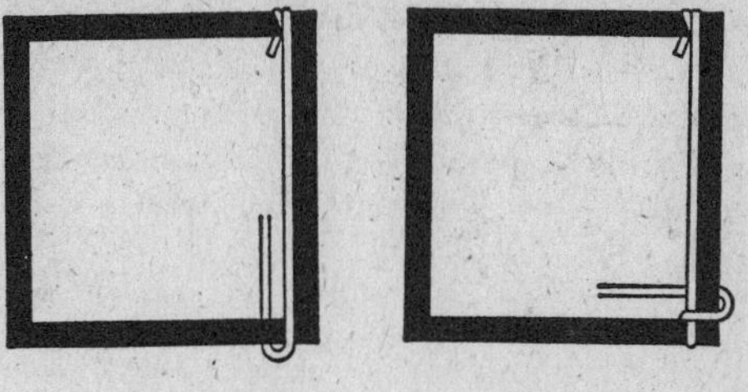

DIAGRAM 2 DIAGRAM 3

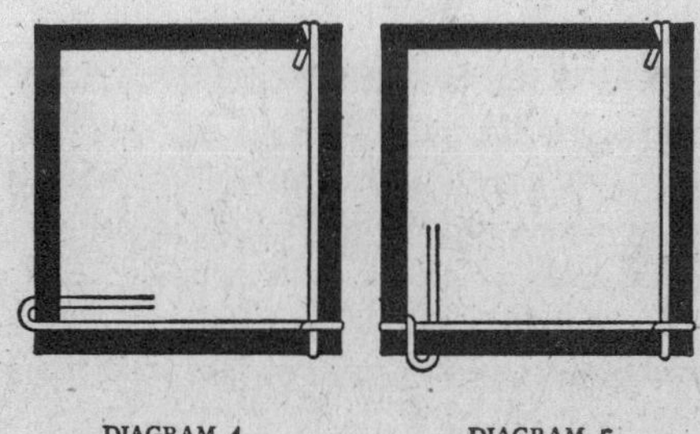

DIAGRAM 4 DIAGRAM 5

DIAGRAM 6

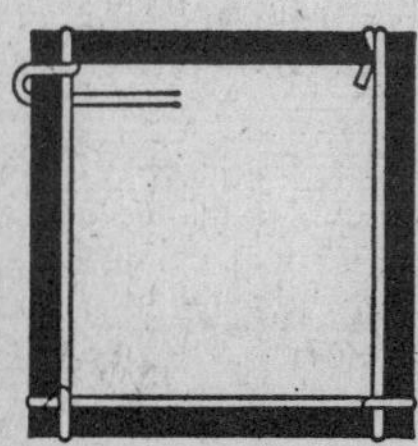

DIAGRAM 7

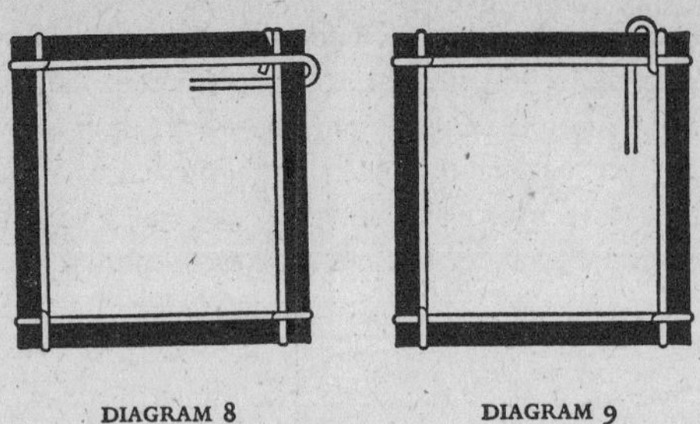

DIAGRAM 8 DIAGRAM 9

You now repeat this process, keeping the tension of the cord as even as possible until the chair is covered. There are two complications which may have to be coped with:

10 The first is that the side rails of a chair are usually longer than the front and back rail. This means that when the front and back rails are full there will still be space on the side rails to be filled before these two triangles are completed. Do this by taking the cord over and under the side rails only, bringing the cord up in the centre each time (diagram 10).

11 The second complication which may arise is that chair seats are rarely square. The front rail tends to be longer than the back rail. Unless you compensate for this you will not be able to get a neat pattern. Mark the front rail at the points where it forms a perfect square with the shorter back rail. The length between the ends of the front rail and these marks must be filled first. Do this by fastening the cord at the right corner of the front rail, tacking the end under

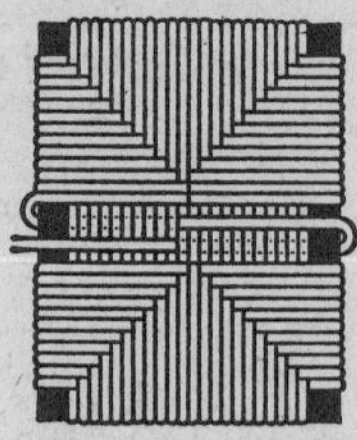

DIAGRAM 10

the frame. Pass the cord over and under the front rail. Now pass it over and under the right rail. Take the cord across the frame and pass it over and under the left-hand rail. Now bring it over and under the front rail, over and under the left rail again and back across the frame. Take the cord over and under the right rail, over and under the front rail, over and under the right rail again and back across the frame. Continue like this until the extra length on the front rail is filled and you have a square shape left to fill. You can then carry on in the usual way using all four sides of the frame (diagrams 11a and 11b).

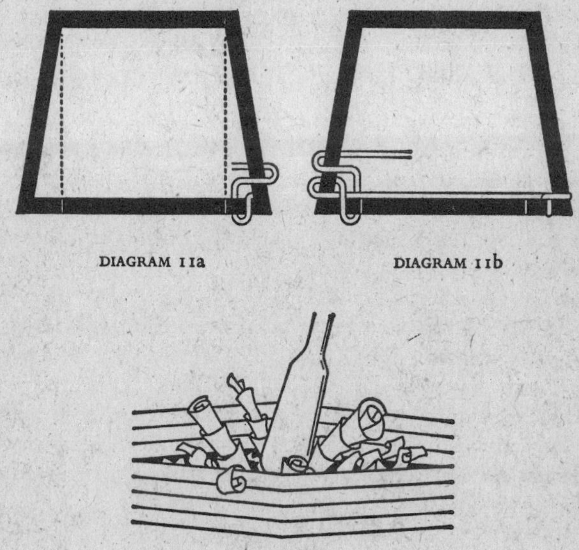

DIAGRAM 11a

DIAGRAM 11b

DIAGRAM 12
Plumping out the seat with extra fibre

12 Fasten off securely by tying and tacking the cord underneath the frame.

13 To give the seat a plumper appearance it is usually stuffed between the weave with twists of paper or scraps of the weaving material itself (diagram 12). Turn the chair upside down and do this from under-

neath. Any blunt, spatula-type instrument can be used for forcing the stuffing between the cords. The same instrument can be used with the chair the right way up to neaten the appearance of the weave and straighten it up if necessary. You can cheat a little with strands that have gone rather crooked by tacking them into the right position on the underside of the frame.

Some types of fibre look good with a coat of clear or golden lacquer and benefit from the protection it gives.

8

China, glass and metals

China

Cleaning

Old china may not be broken but may still require attention because it is dirty; dirt ingrained in hairline cracks in the glaze and old glued repairs can spoil the appearance and make china unusable if it is intended to hold food. There are two main points to remember when cleaning china. One is that very hot water may dissolve old glues which have been used for repairs, and most old china repairs will have been done with water-soluble glue. The other is that some very delicate china may have decoration which will come off if treated with very hot water, bleach or hard rubbing. Bearing this in mind, the best way to clean dirty china is first of all to try a mild solution of washing-up liquid in hand-hot water. Wash up in a soft bowl to avoid the possibility of marking the china further. Using an old toothbrush, scrub along particularly stubborn marks using neat detergent. If you think the decoration can take it you can also try a scouring pad. If this does not work, try adding a small quantity of domestic *bleach* to a fresh solution of washing-up liquid. Always start with a small amount of bleach and increase a little at a time if it does not seem to be working. It is best to increase the time you leave the articles in the solution rather than use too strong a bleach which may affect the china. This is particularly important if you are going to mend the piece as well as clean it, for too much bleach may make it difficult for the adhesive to work properly. Denture cleaner is often an effective stain remover for dirty china.

If there is any difficulty which makes it impossible to immerse the article, cleaning must be done with cloths wrung out in the detergent solution. Bleaching should be done by soaking a pad of cotton or cotton wool in a solution of domestic bleach or hydrogen peroxide.

Wipe this over the stain, and leave a pad of bleach on the affected area, renewing it when it dries out.

Articles should always be rinsed thoroughly with clean water after treatment. Where it is not possible to immerse an object in clean water, rinsing must be done by wiping several times with cloths wrung out in clean water.

If you want to make sure china is *hygienic* for food or drink, then treat it with the solution used for keeping babies' bottles sterile.

Grease is removed with methylated spirit or white spirit (turpentine substitute.)

Mending breaks with adhesives

China used to be mended with metal *rivets* because adhesives were not capable of giving a strong join which could not be dissolved by hot water. The development of modern synthetic adhesives, particularly epoxy adhesives, has made this unnecessary. Indeed one of the jobs you may wish to attempt is the removal of unsightly rivets so that the piece can be given a fresh invisible repair with adhesive. If you are going to remove old rivets, file through them with a metal file and prise them out carefully. You may also wish to *reassemble* old glued repairs which have become unsightly because of discoloration. These will probably come apart when soaked in hot water. If not, try a solvent such as acetone (nail polish remover), surgical spirit, white spirit or methylated spirit. The latter is the only one likely to be effective on a repair done with a modern epoxy adhesive, although usually it will only do a satisfactory job on epoxy adhesive which has not fully set. You will get other ideas from the list of solvents on p. 147ff. DIY shops often sell proprietary glue solvents.

Sometimes a wide crack, which is collecting a lot of grime, is best broken completely and cleaned and mended as for a straightforward fracture. If this does not seem like a good idea then prise the crack apart with a razor blade so that it can be cleaned and repaired as far as possible, according to the method for repairing a clean break given below.

1 *Clean* the edges of the break so that when it is repaired the thin layer of grime does not draw attention to the fault. All solvent and bleach should be rinsed off and the edges to be joined should be totally free of grease.

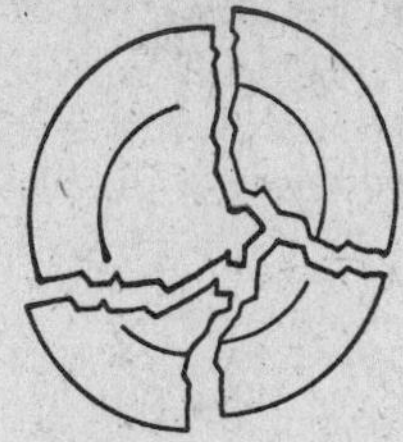

DIAGRAM 1
Work out order of assembly

2 *Fit the pieces together before applying adhesive*, (diagram 1) even for a simple fracture. This is very important if there are several pieces to be joined together as you will then be able to work out the best order for fixing them together. Do not try to glue together more than two pieces at a time. Let each repair dry thoroughly and then fit in the next piece, so that there is no possibility of everything slipping out of line.

3 *Applying pressure*. After you have applied adhesive you should apply pressure to the join to hold the edges together as tightly as possible until the glue has dried. You should work out how you are going to apply this pressure *before* applying the adhesive. Diagrams 2–7 will give you some ideas of how to apply pressure and support to typical repairs.

On a straightforward break, tape should be stuck across the line

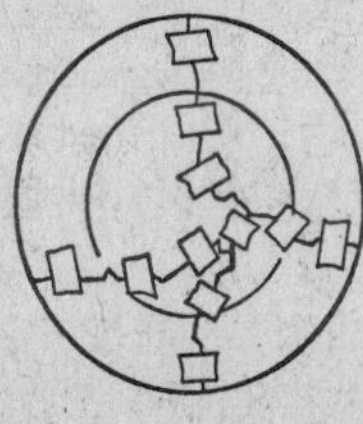

DIAGRAM 2
Using gummed strip

DIAGRAM 3
One plate supports another

of the fracture to draw the two sides together. Running tape along the line of the fracture is virtually useless. For best results use gummed brown paper strip rather than adhesive tape, which tends to stretch and lose its tension after a short time. Gummed strip has the added advantage that it has to be dampened before use and as it dries it shrinks and pulls even tighter across the join.

Even flat joins benefit from additional support such as a sand bed. If you have another identical plate or saucer place the damaged one on it until the adhesive has set. Skilled repairers frequently mould individual supports from plaster or paraffin wax if they have a duplicate to work from. The technique is the same as in moulding replacements (see below).

DIAGRAM 4
Fulcrum method

Each different repair requires a slightly different support but when trying a method out it is a good test to see whether the pieces which are to be mended will stay in position for at least a few seconds simply as a result of the position you have placed them in. Try to make as much use of gravity as possible in the way you incline the pieces, so as to give additional strength to supports such as lumps of plasticine or the sand box. Trial and error will enable you to concoct ingenious supports from the most unlikely items.

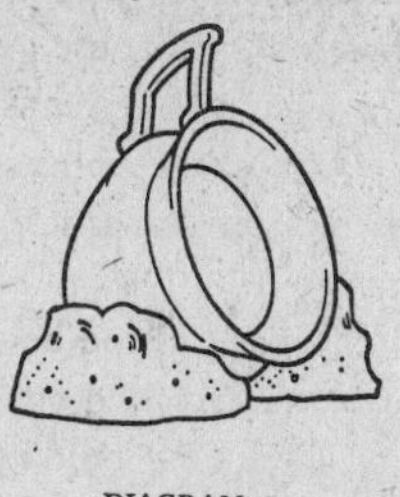

DIAGRAM 5
Plasticine

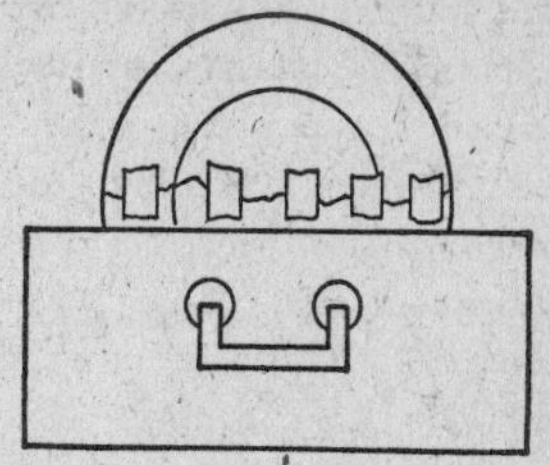

DIAGRAM 6
A plate held straight in a drawer

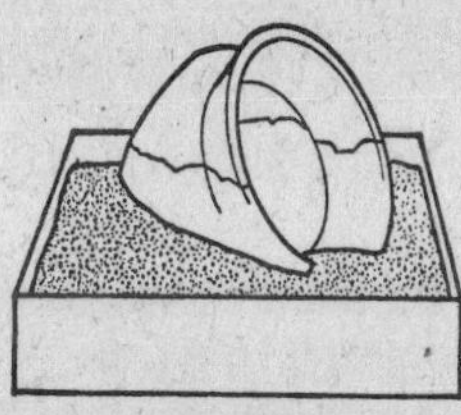

DIAGRAM 7
Sand box

4 *Apply adhesive* when you have worked out the order of building up the repair and the best means of supporting the glued pieces. Use an epoxy adhesive for greatest strength, unless you are very unsure of your skill as a repairer and want to use a glue which is more easily removed for a fresh start. Epoxy adhesives can generally be removed with methylated spirit for up to six hours after application. It is therefore a good idea to check on your repair after three or four hours so that if it has slipped or seems unsatisfactory you still have a chance to start again. Once an epoxy adhesive has dried the only way way to remove it is to chip it off.

Follow the instructions for mixing the glue and hardener which together make up an epoxy adhesive. Mixing should ideally be done on a piece of glass or tile, but this is not essential. Use the spatula, as epoxy adhesive can cause skin irritation. For best results work in a warm atmosphere.

Apply the adhesive as thinly as possible along both sides of the break and press them firmly together. Too much adhesive gives a less efficient repair and one which will be more obvious. When you are mending a multiple fracture it is particularly important to use a minimum of adhesive, as a build-up over several joins will alter the size and shape of the original. Surplus adhesive should be wiped away before it hardens, unless you are using an adhesive with a known solvent. Any type of adhesive which gets on to original gilt decoration should be wiped away immediately as solvents used later may also remove the decoration. Pressure should now be applied as described in 3 above, until the adhesive has dried thoroughly. Resist the temptation to return constantly and look at the repair, as handling is sure to make it move out of true.

A repair placed in a warm atmosphere, such as an airing cupboard, will dry much faster than one left at room temperature, but even so it is best left for several days. If you are really impatient then use one of the fast setting epoxy adhesives now on the market, but remember that this cuts down on the time available for realigning a repair that is not satisfactory at the first attempt. *Heating* in the oven will also speed up the drying time but carries the risk of causing hair line cracks in the glaze and discoloring the adhesive. The temperature should never be greater than 95C (200F) or gas regulo ¼.

Dowelling repairs (diagrams 8 and 9)
Dowelling is sometimes done in conjunction with glueing when you have two fairly solid pieces of china to hold together. For example you could use it to replace a head which has broken from a statue or to stick on a large piece which you have modelled yourself. The basic technique is the same as that given for dowelling repairs in wood (p. 13). For a dowel use a stiff piece of brass wire or a thin brass nail and groove it slightly with a metal file to allow excess adhesive to escape. If the two holes to be drilled cannot be aligned by accurate measurement, drill the first hole in the centre of the largest, most manageable piece, and insert a piece of pencil lead to protrude just beyond the hole. When you hold the two pieces in position the pencil lead will mark the position of the complementary hole in the same way as the brad does when dowelling wood. Use epoxy adhesive or a little plaster of Paris to cement the brass pin, and use adhesive along the flat surfaces of the repair. Missing flakes of glaze and colour

DIAGRAM 8
Strengthening a repair with a dowelling pin

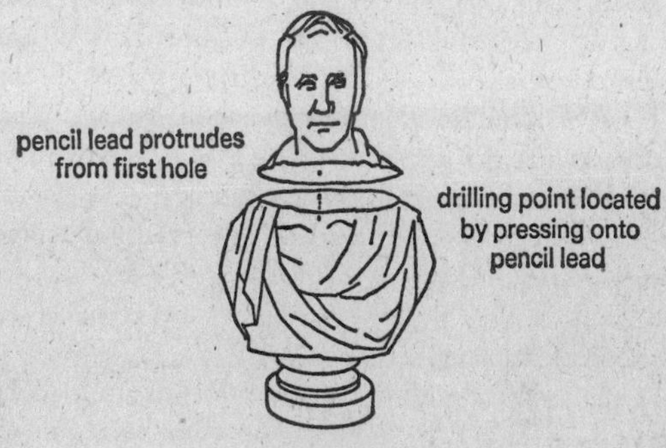

DIAGRAM 9
Marking the drilling points

are almost inevitable along the line of the fracture and these should be repaired using the techniques for filling and redecorating described below.

Filling chips and cracks

Missing chips and flakes are a frequent problem with old china, even if there are no major fractures. Plates for example frequently get chipped at the rim, while being washed. Sometimes these chips are very deep and occasionally they even become small holes in the object. If this is the case the filler will need some additional support until it

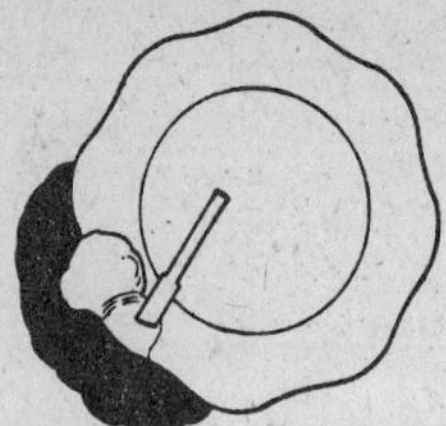
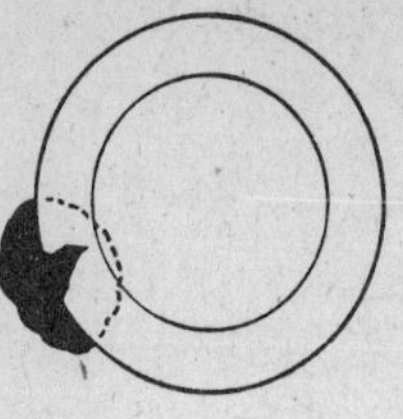

DIAGRAM 10 and 11
Using plasticine as a base for filling chips and holes

has dried. The same technique should be followed for filling holes as for shallow chips, but over a base of plasticine dusted with titanium dioxide, to prevent the filler sticking to it (diagrams 10 and 11).

First the area to be repaired must be thoroughly cleaned and allowed to dry. Next decide on the filler you are going to use. Professional restorers usually make their own, using a mixture of epoxy adhesive into which is worked as much titanium dioxide as the adhesive can be made to absorb. This produces a very white filler, which is a good match for white china and which will also take a surface colour very well. Other similar powders mixed into the epoxy adhesive will produce different coloured fillers which may occasionally be useful to create a match with an unusual colour. French chalk will make a grey filler, and kaolin a biscuit coloured filler. In addition you can mix artists' powder colours with the filler itself to match the colour of the object you are repairing. This is useful if the area is so small it does not warrant repainting and varnishing, or if you are mending unglazed china, where surface painting and varnishing would create the wrong appearance.

If you do not want to make your own filler, or you do not have the skill to handle the rather sticky filler which results from making one of the epoxy putties, you can buy ready-made china modelling pastes/fillers. One of the best known is the type made popular by the craze for Barbola modelling work in the 1920's. These modelling pastes are readily available from artists' supply shops under a variety of different trade names, and most of them can be mixed with artists' powder colours like an epoxy putty. Barbola itself is water-soluble and should not be used to repair china which will be used and washed.

Work filler into the crack or chip using a finger or a penknife. Overfill slightly to allow for shrinkage when the filler dries out. Any moulding or shaping, on the edge of a plate for example, should be copied as accurately as possible. If epoxy putty starts to dry out before this is satisfactorily completed, dip the tool you are working with into a little methylated spirit to restore the putty's flexibility. Proprietary fillers should be moistened with a little of the solvent recommended in the maker's instructions.

After about twelve hours the putty will have set sufficiently for the excess to be removed. Use a razor to scrape away large amounts, and a piece of finest grade dampened 'wet and dry' paper for the final smoothing. On Barbola paste use a dry paper. Be careful not to rub over any adjacent decoration.

Moulding and modelling (Advanced)

When pieces of broken china are missing you may like to make your own replacements. The simplest way of doing this is to take a cast or pressing from an identical piece and use it to fashion a copy in modelling paste/filler or plaster of Paris. Pressing is the method used for making replacements which are more or less flat. Moulding is used to make an impression of a three-dimensional section such as an arm or handle.

The theory of making replacements in both these ways is relatively simple but a good deal of experience and skill is needed to judge the type of mould required and the best material from which to make it. For example, a mould for a simple piece like a plain knob can be made in a substance such as plaster of Paris, which sets hard. Where a replacement is more complex, particularly if it is not completely solid, then a cast should be made with material which sets to a more malleable consistency. This makes it easier to remove without damaging the original from which the mould is being taken. Materials for making moulds can generally be obtained from good artists' supply shops and craft shops. The material used by dentists for copying teeth is also a very good material for making moulds, as is paraffin wax.

Pressings

Diagrams 12 and 13 show how to make a pressing of the edge of a plate. The material used for taking the pressing is plasticine, which

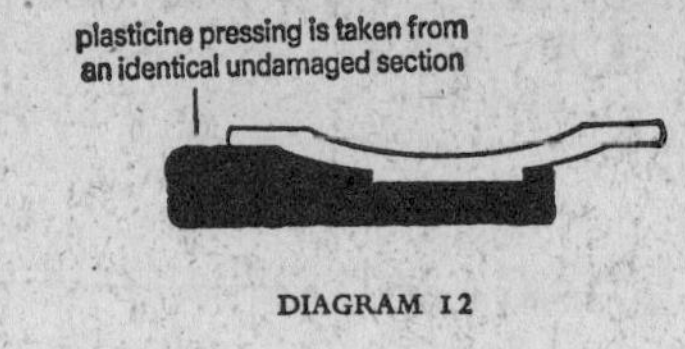

DIAGRAM 12

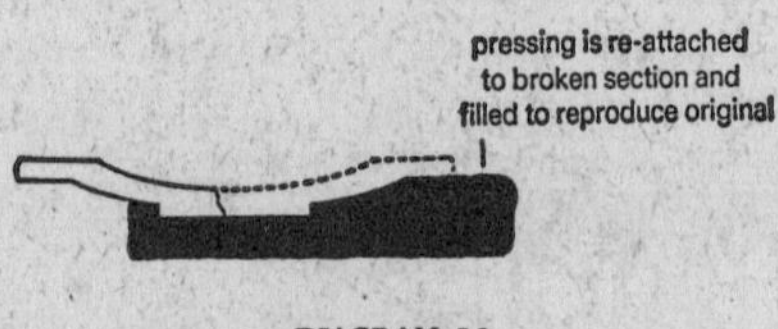

DIAGRAM 13

should be kneaded until it is soft and smooth and then rolled out to a thickness of about 1 cm. (Warm paraffin wax can be used instead of plasticine.) The plasticine is then moulded around a section which duplicates the missing section. This area should first be moistened with cold water so that the pressing will slip off easily without any distortion. You should allow about 2 cm of overlap on all sides so that the pressing can be reattached to the plate around the missing section.

Remove the pressing and fit it where the original is missing. The plasticine shape should then be filled with a modelling paste/filler. You can use a ready-mixed filler such as Barbola paste or you can make up your own epoxy putty as described on page 120. The disadvantage of epoxy putty is its stickiness. If it seems to be sticking to the plasticine pressing, dust the plasticine with titanium dioxide. If epoxy putty gets rather too stiff to fill the pressing without fear of distorting the plasticine, moisten it with a little methylated spirit. Epoxy putty and proprietary modelling pastes can be coloured with artists' powder colours if desired.

You can model the replacement piece in such a way that it adheres automatically to the original plate. However you may find it easier to model the replacement first and then glue it in as if making a repair with adhesive (p. 114). Either way the pressing should be left until it has set really hard (at least twelve hours). Always err on the side of making the replacement a little too large; any excess can then be adjusted when you give the new part a fine shaping with moistened fine grade 'wet and dry' glass paper. Use a dry paper on Barbola paste.

Moulds

Diagrams 14–18 show how a basic rigid mould is made. Flexible moulds are made in the same way but the rubbery substance makes oiling the china unnecessary. Most moulds are made in two parts although this is not always essential. If the piece from which you are taking the mould is still attached to something else, for instance if you are matching up a missing handle on a soup tureen, you will first have to experiment to find the best way of positioning the piece so

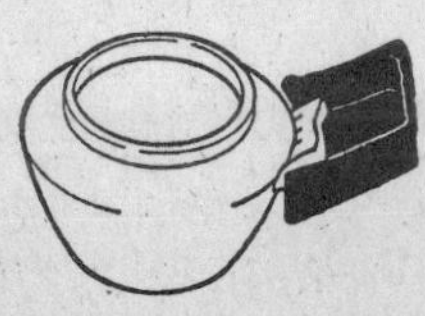

DIAGRAM 14
Plasticine box is built up round undamaged handle from which cast is to be taken

DIAGRAM 15
Plasticine box is supported in sand box and half filled with Plaster of Paris

that the mould can be built around it. Obviously the piece to be modelled must be in a container which will hold the material from which the mould is to be made. You should be able to buy little rubber or plastic containers for this purpose from shops which supply other modelling materials. Alternatively you can make a 'box' yourself from plasticine. If the container is to go round one section of a larger object then you will probably have to make a plasticine box yourself in order to get the right shape (diagram 15).

Make up plaster of Paris and fill the container to a convenient point for dividing the mould (usually about half way). The section you are taking the cast from should first be brushed with a little oil so that the plaster of Paris does not stick to it when it dries. When this first half of the cast has set, the second half can be poured on (diagram 16).

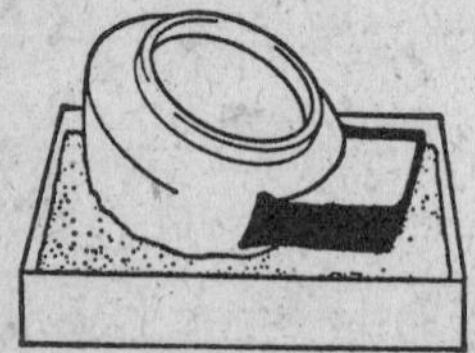

DIAGRAM 16
First half of mould is brushed with oil and second half poured on

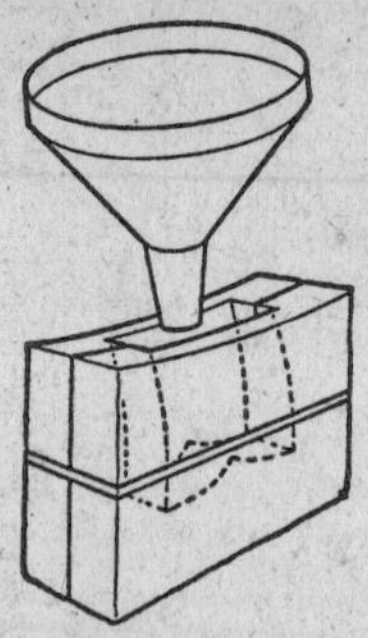

DIAGRAM 17
Two sides of mould securely joined and filled with Plaster of Paris

This time the edges of the first half of the cast should also be brushed with oil so that it will be easy to separate the two halves and remove them without damaging the original.

The replacement section is made by filling this mould with plaster of Paris or epoxy putty or Barbola paste. The inside of the mould should be rubbed with a parting agent such as a beeswax polish before use, so that the modelling material will not stick to the mould.

If the new piece is to be cast by filling with a substance which has a pouring consistency, such as plaster of Paris, the two halves of the mould are secured together and the filler is poured in and left to set. You must therefore make a mould with a hole to allow the filler in. The simplest way to do this is to make sure that the end of the piece from which you are taking the cast abuts the wall of the plasticine 'box', so that it does not get closed over. Therefore, if you are making the mould from a separate piece or from a pattern which you have modelled yourself from plasticine, pin this to the side of the plasticine 'box' before making the mould (diagram 18).

If this is impossible, and you cannot find another convenient area to allow a hole for pouring in the filler, then the replacement piece should be made with epoxy putty or a proprietary modelling paste.

When using this type of filler the two halves of the mould are filled separately and then pressed and held together securely until the filler

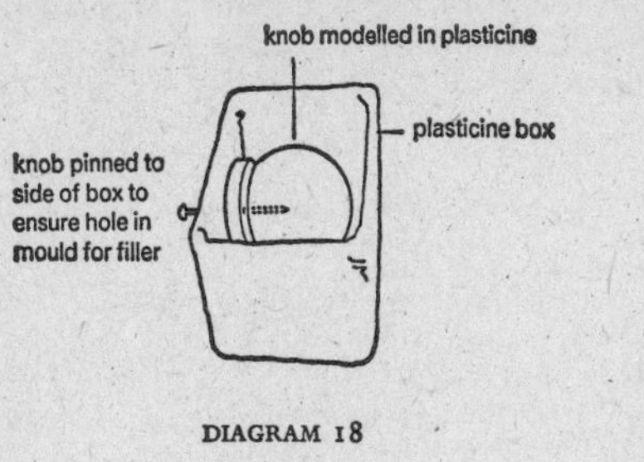

DIAGRAM 18

DIAGRAM 19
Finished jar

has hardened. Since it is not possible to judge accurately the exact amount of filler needed for each half, the two halves are overfilled and the excess which is squeezed out when they are fitted together is allowed to escape along grooves cut into the adjacent surfaces of the mould (diagram 20). It is therefore important when using this type of filler to coat the grooves and the adjacent edges of the mould as well as the shape itself with the parting agent. If you fail to do this the two sides of the mould will stick together and the cast will probably get broken when the mould is forced apart.

Finish the newly moulded section by abrading with fine sandpaper. Use adhesive to stick it into place, then decorate. Replacement sections can be strengthened by a wire core. For basic method see diagrams 21–23 for moulding a replacement cup handle.

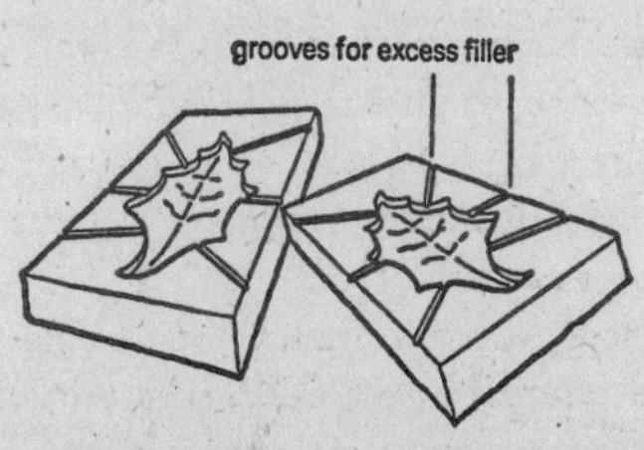

DIAGRAM 20
Mould for thick filler

DIAGRAM 21
Mould for cup handle

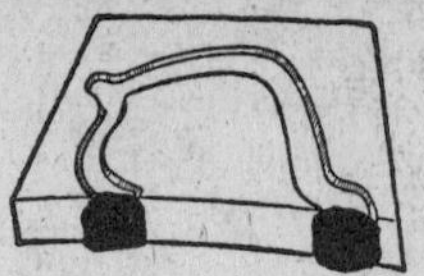

DIAGRAM 22
Mould is part filled

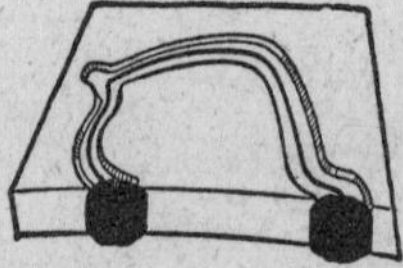

DIAGRAM 23
Wire core is placed in mould before remaining filler is poured on

Modelling

If you do not have a suitable copy from which to make a mould, if the missing pieces of china are too small to model (small leaves and flowers, for example) or if you have a great deal of artistic flair, you may wish to make freehand models of missing pieces of china. Modelling can be done with proprietary modelling paste, or with epoxy putty. Either of these can be coloured with artists' powder pigments. If the paste gets too dry or sticky, moisten it with the manufacturer's recommended solvent. Methylated spirit on your fingers or the tools

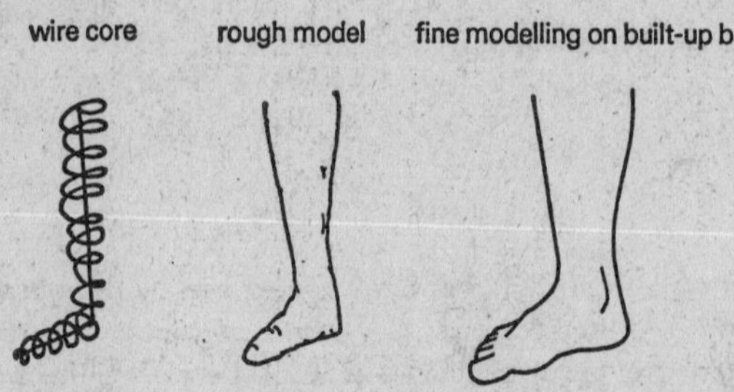

DIAGRAM 24

you are using will help keep epoxy putty from hardening too quickly. Large pieces should be strengthened by a wire core (diagram 24). This will probably necessitate building up several layers of the modelling paste and allowing them to form a base before doing the fine modelling itself on a final layer.

An alternative to modelling directly in epoxy putty or filler is to model in a more malleable material such as plasticine and make a pressing or mould as described above.

Redecorating china repairs

As with modelling, a lot of your success with redecorating will depend on basic artistic skill. Unglazed ware can be imitated fairly satisfactorily by mixing artists' powder paints into the filler you use. Surface colour for glazed ware is largely a matter of trial and error. Artists' supply shops stock proprietary brands of paint suitable for china, which usually have a complementary varnish to simulate the protective glaze. Alternatively you can make up your own by mixing artists' powder colours with clear picture varnish. The picture varnish acts as a size which prevents the paint from sinking into the filler which has been used to mend the original. Paints which imitate real gilt are readily available from artists' supply shops. One of the best, although rather expensive, is American Treasure Gold Liquid Leaf. It is very poisonous and should be stored well out of the reach of children and pets.

When the redecoration is dry it can be varnished with a clear lacquer to simulate the glaze. A polyurethane is quite adequate and best if you want a waterproof repair. For really good quality work it is worth testing out the effects of colour and varnish on a separate patch of filler, to see if the final results will match the original.

Glass

Cleaning

Straightforward washing of glassware should always be done in a soft plastic bowl to prevent damage. If the tap cannot be moved to one side, protect that too with some sort of plastic collar. Use a mild solution of water and detergent. The water should never be more than lukewarm. You are almost bound to crack the glass if you change the temperature of the water quickly. Dry with a lint-free cloth and polish if desired with a chamois leather. Glass that is stored damp will become cloudy. You can prevent this happening by drying the inside of narrow-necked containers with a hairdryer set at a cool heat. If containers with stoppers are being stored, the stoppers should be kept separately, to prevent moisture being trapped inside.

Interior sediment stains which do not respond to ordinary washing methods may have eaten into the glass itself or formed a hard crust. An old toothbrush or baby's bottle brush, or an improvised pad on the end of a knitting needle may help to dislodge them. There are now proprietary stain removers on the market which are intended for just this problem and stain removers for dentures also work well. If these do not work, you could try soaking the stained container for two or three days in distilled water (available from chemists or garages) and then scrubbing it again.

Persistent staining will need a mild chemical treatment. Try a solution of distilled water and a mild acid such as vinegar or lemon juice. This should be left covered for at least two days and then the container should be washed again. If staining persists but is lighter repeat the treatment, increasing the strength of the acid. If there is no appreciable difference the stain may respond to the opposite treatment – alkali. Try leaving a mild solution of distilled water and washing soda in the container for a couple of days.

A glazier or jeweller may be prepared to burn off a layer of damaged glass that does not respond to this treatment, with a stronger acid. All chemicals and solvents should be thoroughly rinsed off after use.

Dull glass is probably covered with small scratches. This may well be true of glass which has been treated with acid or alkali to remove persistent staining. Brighten glass with a proprietary window cleaner, which has a mild abrasive action to make the surface of the glass flow together over the scratches. If this mild glass cleaner does not work well enough increase the strength of the abrasive by trying jeweller's rouge applied on a soft cloth or, stronger still, a paste metal polish. Finally wash in warm water and polish dry.

Glass which remains dull in spite of these treatments can be given an imitation sparkle with a coat of transparent lacquer, although this will not stand up to close scrutiny. An alternative used by people who display old glass is to rub olive oil into the surface of the glass and polish it hard. This has a temporary effect.

Cloudy milky glass has probably been stored in damp conditions (see above). One method of dealing with this problem, although no treatment is likely to be totally effective, is to add a 5 per cent solution of ammonia to the water in which you wash the glass. The strength of the solution can be increased a little if necessary. Where cloudiness has affected the interior of a container you can also try shaking a mixture of fine sand and warm water around inside fairly vigorously, as though cleaning a milk bottle. Add ammonia to the solution as well if you think it will help.

Ammonia will also add sparkle to undamaged glass. If you are using ammonia (or mild acid) on *stained glass*, do not let it get onto the lead framework. All chemicals should be rinsed off with clean water afterwards. If, after trying these methods, the cloudiness still persists, the only solution is the temporary one of a hard polish with a little olive oil (see above).

Grease and smears will come off glass with methylated spirit. This should not be used on glass which is surrounded by French polished wood as it will act as a solvent on the polish.

Mirrors

These can be cleaned in any of the ways described above, but be careful not to let acids or solvents damage the frame. *Flymarking* should come off with a solution of approximately one part caustic soda to nineteen parts water. Wash the solution off thoroughly. Protect your hands with waterproof gloves. Use old newspapers to clean off polish and solvents, it leaves no fluff.

Mirrors which look dark and dingy after cleaning may need resilvering. This can usually be done by a glazier. However some old mirrors lose their value when resilvered. If in doubt get professional advice before having an antique mirror resilvered.

Removing stoppers

Jammed stoppers should never be forced out as this will probably break the neck of the container. Lubricate round the top with a mixture of approximately two parts alcohol (methylated spirit), one part glycerine or olive oil and one part table salt. Use a thin paint brush to get the mixture as far down the neck of the container as possible, leave overnight and then ease the stopper out gently. Gentle heating over a radiator, for example, or with a cool hairdryer for a few minutes, will expand the air inside the container and help push the stopper out. Never try any stronger heat or the glass will crack.

Riveting (Advanced)

This is strictly a job for professionals and usually unnecessary these days because modern adhesives give adequate strength to a repair, especially when it is for display purposes only.

Adhesives

Cracked glass can be mended with adhesives in the same way as china (p. 114). Wipe the edges thoroughly with methylated spirit and allow to dry so that the adhesive has every chance of working efficiently. Epoxy adhesives give a strong repair, and are essential if the piece is likely to be immersed in water later on. If a piece is for display only a celluloid adhesive gives a clearer and less visible repair than an epoxy resin, which tends to go cloudy after a while.

Dowelling (Advanced)

Broken stems can be repaired by the dowelling method on the same principles as wood (p. 13) and china (p. 118). As a dowel use a measured piece of thin glass rod, available from a glazier, with the clearest possible adhesive. Use a very narrow bit on a hand drill and drill very slowly. The chances are that drilling will shatter the glass completely and dowelling repairs on valuable glass should always be taken to an expert.

Filling chips and cracks

This can be done in the same way as for china (p. 119). The material to use is the liquid plastic used for making paperweights *etc.* which is generally available from artist's supply shops and craft shops. These liquid plastics are usually clear but can be coloured if you wish to match coloured glass. Unless the manufacturer's instructions advise otherwise use artists' oils for colouring.

Chips in the edge of glass can be ground down. You can do this yourself if you have a grinding machine for lapidary work. Valuable glass should always be ground professionally.

Repairing enamel

Enamel is opaque glass which has been fused onto a metal base. Like china it cannot be refired so repairs have to imitate the real thing. You can do this with an epoxy putty coloured with artists' powder colours (see Filling chips and cracks in china, p. 119). This can be given a coat of polyurethane varnish afterwards for a glossy appearance. Very small defects can be camouflaged by a little coloured wax, such as candle wax, available from artists' supply shops and craft shops. This can be ready-coloured or you can colour it yourself. You may also be able to find in the same type of shop kits for making up plastic enamel brooches *etc.* which make very good repairs as they dry hard without being fired.

Silver

Cleaning

Both silver and silver plate can be treated in the same way, although you must be careful not to use too strong an abrasive on very thin plate—not all silver plate is of equal quality. All silver is soft, and the purer the alloy the softer the metal, so do not be tempted to use a harsh material like wire wool to remove tarnish.

First try a *good wash* in warm, soapy water followed by thorough drying and polishing with a soft cloth or chamois leather. This is a good follow-up procedure if you have already used a polish or chemical on the silver. If washing does not work try one of the many proprietary silver polishes on the market. These polishes have an abrasive action which removes a fine skin of the metal to reveal clean metal underneath. It is therefore best to choose a polish which professes to have a long-lasting effect so that you do not wear away the silver more than necessary.

Chased and patterned silver may trap silver polish. This should be washed off or its chemical action will continue to eat away at the metal. Bearing in mind that much chased silver is intended to be left black in the grooves to emphasise the pattern, you can try cleaning with a soft brush to get the polish in and out of the nooks and crannies.

An alternative to standard metal polish which works well on intricate pieces of metalwork is a proprietary chemical cleaner, usually called a 'silver dip'. The article is immersed in this chemical solution which removes a fine surface layer of metal.

Very dirty or delicate silver can be taken to a jeweller for electrochemical cleaning, a chemical process which does not damage the metal. An old-fashioned method of doing this is often recommended by restorers—the aluminium method. Place crumpled-up aluminium foil in the bottom of an enamel basin. Place the silver articles on the aluminium and fill the bowl with a 5–10 per cent solution of water and washing soda. This will create a chemical reaction accompanied by a lot of foaming and bubbling. Since fumes are created it is best to work out of doors or in a well ventilated room. After a minute or two, when the reaction has died down, remove the articles with tongs, wash them well in a mild soapy solution, dry thoroughly and polish with a chamois leather or a soft cloth. Do not use chemical cleaners on silverplate which has worn through to the base metal.

Really bad tarnish, which may also be accompanied by corrosion and pitting, should be treated with a solution of approximately 1 part ammonia to 9 parts distilled water. The article should be left to soak for a day or two. This will halt the corroding process. The solution should then be properly rinsed off with clean water and the article dried and polished with a soft cloth. Failure to do this will eventually lead to damage from traces of the ammonia itself. Very bad patches of tarnish can be treated with neat ammonia which should then be properly rinsed off. Ammonia gives off fumes and should be used outside or in a well ventilated room. Protect your hands with waterproof gloves.

Preventing tarnish and corrosion

Correct care and storage of silver will prevent damage. One obvious method is to varnish with a clear metal varnish when you have achieved a good lustre. This is sometimes done to silver which is to be put on display, or where too much repolishing will damage soft metal. However it can sometimes detract from the appearance. Frequent use of anti-tarnish cloths should make it unnecessary to polish too often. Really good quality silver should be stored in separate felt bags. Black plastic bags are a cheaper substitute.

Damp has a very harmful effect on silver, as do salt (including sea air) and chemical pollution. Take care to protect silver from fresh paint fumes. Silver containers, especially those used for holding salt, should have glass liners. Silver vases should also have glass liners if they are going to be used to hold flowers. Do not keep silver cutlery in bundles held together by rubber bands as this causes damage to the metal.

Mending

Because silver is so soft one of the commonest mending problems is straightening out the small dents which are known as 'bruising'. You can try gently knocking these back into shape with a rubber hammer or even with your fingers (diagram 1) if the metal is soft enough. If this does not work it is best to take the silver to an expert.

Scratches can be removed by polishing with jeweller's rouge on a soft cloth or chamois leather. Swansdown rouge, an even finer abrasive, can then be used for a final buffing. Careful use of a polishing attachment on an electric drill will quickly bring up a shine.

Small holes and cracks in silver which has worn thin can be repaired and camouflaged. This should not be done on anything of real value. The filling can be done with epoxy putty (p. 120) which can be coloured silver or left plain and painted over afterwards. You can also use a proprietary filler such as plastic padding (sometimes called 'cold solder'). These can then be disguised with a good quality silver paint or wax such as the ones in the American Treasure Gold range, available from art shops. To get the lustre as well as the colour of silver these imitation colours should be painted over with a varnish in the same range. When filling all but the tiniest cracks, back the gap with some sort of masking tape and build the filler up over it (diagram 2). Such repairs will be suitable for display only.

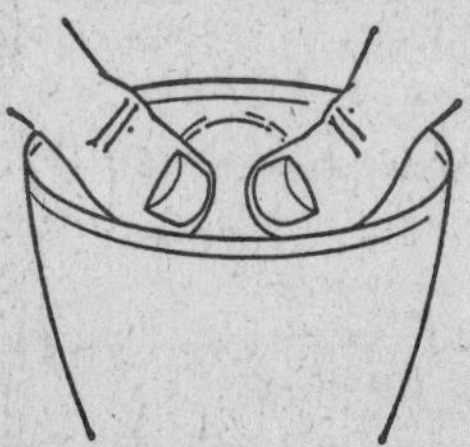

DIAGRAM 1
Pressing out 'bruised' silver

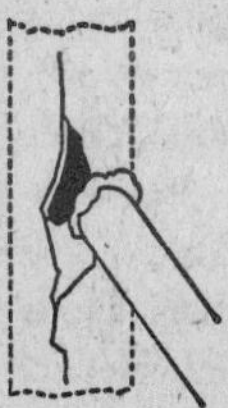

DIAGRAM 2
Back filler with masking tape

Broken silver of any real value should be taken to an expert to be soldered. If you have some experience of soldering you may like to mend items yourself. If so, remember that soft solder contains lead and should not be used on silver as it will cause corrosion.

Epoxy adhesives can, in theory, be used for sticking metal, including silver. However results are often disappointing.

Worn plate can be replated. If you are buying something with the idea of replating make sure it is not cracked or split in any way as this may make replating impossible. You may find it easier, and certainly cheaper, to disguise small blemishes with a silver paint or paste.

Copper and brass

These two metals can be given the same treatment. Brass is an alloy of copper and zinc.

Cleaning

There are plenty of proprietary cleaners on the market which will deal with a normal level of dirt and tarnish. Slightly worse cases can be effectively treated with a mild acid, such as lemon juice or vinegar, combined with salt. It is most important to rinse off all traces of this (and any other cleaner you use), as the chemicals will continue to eat at the metal when they have finished with the tarnish. After rinsing, dry thoroughly or the metal will darken again.

A solution of approximately 1 part ammonia to 9 parts water will give sparkle to the metal and will also treat tarnish if the object is left to soak in it. You may be able to save on effort by washing articles in warm soapy water with a dash of ammonia before cleaning with a polish. Remember to keep the work area well ventilated to prevent a build-up of ammonia fumes, and protect your hands. Rinse and dry thoroughly after treating with ammonia solution.

Some brass and copper objects which have been subject to adverse conditions, in smoky kitchens for instance, may have such a thick layer of tarnish that they are virtually unrecognisable. All but the most delicate of these can be given a coat of rust remover (the sort used on cars) which should be left until the true colour of the metal begins to show through. For really bad cases a metal scouring pad can also be used. The rust remover must then be thoroughly rinsed off and the shine brought up with a proprietary polish. A polishing attachment on an electric drill is a great help here.

Elaborately decorated brass work, such as Oriental Benares ware, should be cleaned out with a stiff brush to get rid of dirty deposits. However do not try and clean away the *patina* in the crevices so that surface and recesses are of equal brightness. The surface is intended to be brighter, so that the contrast creates interest.

If you find you are having no success cleaning brass and copper, it has probably been protected with a lacquer and this must be cleaned away with a proprietary paint stripper before polishing will have any effect.

Brass is often found on wooden furniture. When cleaning these brass fittings remove them from the wood if at all possible, as brass polish will damage the surrounding wood. If the brasswork cannot be taken off, protect the adjacent areas with masking tape or a cardboard frame (diagrams 3 and 4).

DIAGRAM 3
Masking tape keeps metal polish off wood

DIAGRAM 4
Cardboard frame round brass handle keeps metal polish off wood

When you have cleaned brass and copper articles you may prefer to lacquer them rather than keep them clean by repolishing. If they are going to be kept in a damp atmosphere such as a kitchen this is the best method. However, good quality items, particularly those made of brass, should be allowed to develop a gentle patina and this will not be possible if they are lacquered over. Some brass items are of extremely high quality, unlike the more common or garden pots and pans and fireside tools. If you have something of this type do not lacquer it, but keep it clean by giving it an occasional rub over with a soft cloth dipped in paraffin and jeweller's rouge.

Mending

Major damage should be taken to an expert for resoldering. Small holes can be filled with a filler of the type used for patching holes in car bodywork and then disguised with a copper or brass finish. If necessary build up the filler over a base of masking tape. This type of repair will improve the appearance, although only resoldering will give a watertight finish.

Changing the colour

Unfortunately repairing and cleaning can make brass and copper look like new, and a bright, harsh colour is sometimes as bad as tarnish. You can give a more subtle tone to these metals by soaking them in a solution of ammonium sulphide. The stronger the solution and the more prolonged the soaking the darker the colour will be. Rinse and dry thoroughly after soaking. To preserve the new shade give the metal a coat of clear varnish.

Iron

Much ironwork is decorative as well as solid and repays the effort it usually takes to clean off rust and old paint and give a new finish.

Cleaning

Although iron, particularly cast iron, can be rather brittle and prone to damage while being repaired, it can also take a lot of harsh treatment when being cleaned. You do not have to worry about scratches as you do with the softer metals, so you can use a wire brush. Otherwise a vigorous scrub with wire wool (or a soap-filled scouring pad under running water if the article is small enough) can be used to wash off rust. It is essential to get rid of all patches of rust before refinishing, as any rust remaining under a fresh finish will continue to spread. This is important to remember with garden furniture, which tends to get rusty around the feet. It is tempting to assume that this can be left, but if you do so a new finish will soon deteriorate again. Really bad cases can be treated with a preparation intended to remove rust on car bodywork. Anything which does not yield to this type of treatment must be chipped out. Damage on a visible area should then be filled with iron cement (see below) before refinishing.

Old paint and lacquer will come off easily with a proprietary paint stripper.

Mending and refinishing

Metal can be stuck to metal with an epoxy adhesive. Make sure the edges to be joined are clean and free of rust and grease. The pieces must be kept together securely until the adhesive has set.

If the object is made of cast iron you will find that it is extremely brittle and liable to snap in spite of its apparent strength. Repairs to very large cast iron articles will probably require welding. (Drilling holes to take a strengthening plate will probably only cause the metal to split.) Welding cast iron is strictly a job for an experienced professional.

Small holes and blemishes can be filled and then camouflaged with paint or polish. You can use a special iron cement, available fr m hardware and DIY shops, or the type of filler used for repairing car bodywork. For more delicate items you can make up your own epoxy putty and colour it with artists' powder paints (p. 120).

Cleaned iron should be sealed with a clear metal varnish, and this often makes an interesting finish in itself. However, iron is usually painted. Ordinary paint will do, though you can buy paint made specially for painting metal. Whichever you choose you will get a better finish if you apply an undercoat of metal primer first.

If you want to make iron look like a more expensive metal, it can be finished with artificial gilding. For small areas use a good quality imitation gilt such as American Treasure Gold. For large objects a metal colour paint spray is the easiest method.

Converting containers to lamps

Almost anything solid is suitable for conversion to a lamp—tin cans, candlesticks, large lumps of stone or driftwood, old-fashioned food and drink containers. The cheapest containers to convert to lamps are old bottles; these can be left plain but they offer an ideal opportunity for trying out different methods of decoration. They can be painted with freehand designs using emulsion paint or paints intended specifically for use on china or glass which are available from most good art shops. Glass can also be decorated with découpage (p. 62) or covered with a mosaic of small stones, mirrors or tiles, set in a special type of cement. These materials are available from lapidary supply shops. Bottles can be filled with coloured liquid (in which case an *exterior* flex must be used both for safety and to avoid leakage) or with attractive stones or marbles. Filling the bottle is a particularly good idea if it is rather light, as it is essential for the lamp to be as stable as possible to avoid accidents.

The electrical part of the conversion, the bulb socket and on/off switch, can be bought as a kit from most electrical stores. You are most likely to need the type designed to wedge into the neck of a container (diagram 1). However if you do wish to convert something solid you can buy a lamp socket kit which has a screw-on base for fixing to flat surfaces (diagram 2).

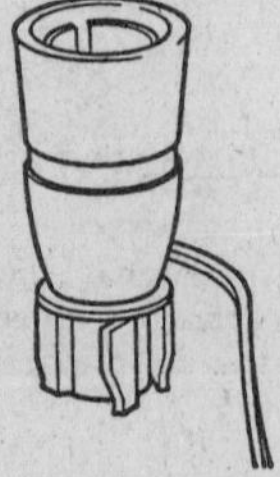

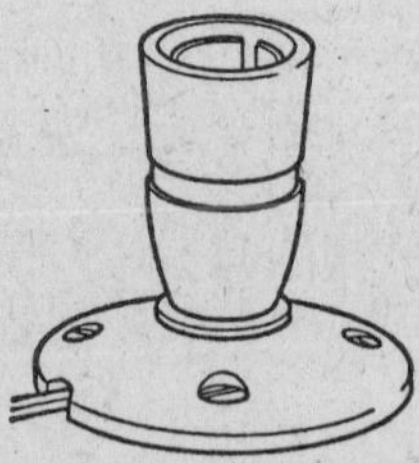

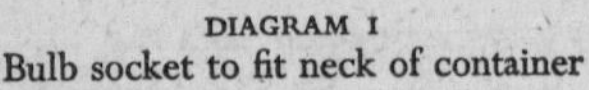

DIAGRAM 1
Bulb socket to fit neck of container

DIAGRAM 2
Bulb socket to screw onto flat surface

Method

The container should be thoroughly cleaned and dried. Any decoration or refinishing except filling the bottle should be done at this stage.

If you are going to run the flex through the container a hole must be drilled just above the base for the flex to emerge. Wherever possible this method is better than an exterior flex because it is more stable. To drill the hole it is best to use a hand drill, over which you have more control than a power drill. Begin with a small bit and increase the size to enlarge the hole in stages. The container should be held firm (diagram 3) while you are drilling. If you have a bottle cutter this will usually have a jig for holding the bottle which will also be suitable for holding a container while you are drilling. If the container you are working on is of glass it is a sensible precaution to protect your eyes against splinters of glass. If the hole you have drilled for the flex has sharp edges which might cut through the wire, the flex must be given extra protection at this point with tape. Alternatively you can buy a rubber eyelet (sometimes called a grummet) from an electrical shop to fit into the hole itself (diagram 4). If the

DIAGRAM 3
Bottle held firmly in jig while hole is drilled

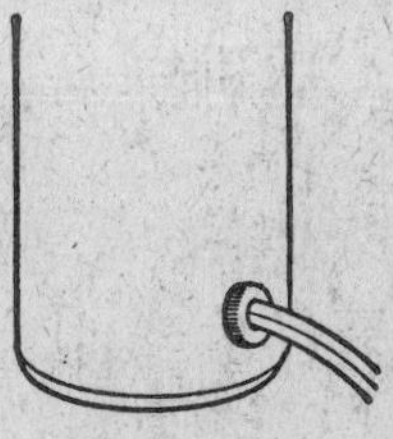

DIAGRAM 4
Rubber grummet protects flex from sharp edges

container you are converting is metal then this is an essential precaution to prevent the danger of cutting into the flex and 'shorting'.

The bulb socket in a standard lamp conversion kit should wedge firmly into the neck of the container. Where the neck is a little too large you can pack plastic padding round the socket to get a secure fit. Where the neck is very wide you can fix the socket into a cork which fits tightly into the neck or make a circular wooden disc to fit across the neck, into which you cut a hole for the socket. If you are using a screw-on type socket on a base which is not made of wood, you will probably have to secure it with an epoxy adhesive and ignore the screws.

9

Materials for special care

Marble

Marble is a form of limestone and is extremely porous. In spite of being hard to the touch it easily absorbs stains to a great depth—a valuable piece of marble should *not* be used as an *ad hoc* coffee table. Any spills, especially wine and all forms of acid, should be wiped up immediately. Marble objects in good condition need no further attention than frequent dusting with a soft cloth.

General cleaning

Cleaning will remove any patina which has built up on the marble. On old pieces this patina may contribute to the value, so consider what you want to achieve before you opt for perfect cleanliness. White marble can be washed with pure soap and water worked up to a lather with a medium hard brush. Rinse well using a soft white cloth or chamois leather (anything else may transfer unwanted colour to such a porous material) and dry quickly and thoroughly. If the marble is really grubby (from a sooty fireplace, for example), add up to 5 per cent ammonia to the washing water.

Coloured marble may be harmed by soap and water. Test a small area before proceeding. Alternative safe cleaning agents for coloured marble, which also can be used on white marble, are petrol, alcohol, acetone, and the proprietary dry-cleaning fluids sold for spot-cleaning textiles. These should be applied on a pad of white cloth and left long enough to give them a chance to work. Afterwards they should be wiped off with a damp white cloth or chamois leather.

Removing stains

Organic stains such as coffee, tea, rust, and stains resulting from damp or fungus, can usually be successfully removed with hydrogen peroxide bleach. The addition of a few drops of ammonia to the solution will make it even more effective. Since marble is so porous the stain may be quite deep, so give the bleach time to penetrate before rinsing off. (If you have added ammonia wait for the bubbling to stop.) Repeat the bleaching process until the stain has disappeared or until you think it is adversely affecting the colour of the marble.

The poultice method is very effective for drawing out stains. If you are treating stains on a vertical surface of something which cannot be moved, such as a garden statue, you will need to use the poultice method to ensure that the bleach works in the right place. Make the poultice by mixing kaolin or whiting to a stiff paste with water. You can make it extra-effective by mixing it with hydrogen peroxide or one of the solvents such as acetone listed above. If there is grease or oil in the stain (usually a dark stain getting progressively paler towards the edges) add one of the solvents already mentioned, or white spirit. Apply the poultice about 2 cm thick to the affected area, allow it to dry, brush it off and rinse away the residue with a damp white cloth or chamois leather. You may need several applications.

Acid is extremely harmful to marble as it dissolves it. However, this dissolving action makes it possible to remove a stained layer of marble, a measure which should only be used as a last resort. The treatment usually recommended is a 5 per cent solution of oxalic acid. This is extremely poisonous and you may have difficulty obtaining it. Never use it near children or pets and rinse the solution off into a container so that it can be safely disposed of. Some proprietary rust removers, which contain acid, will have a similar effect. Any acid treatment should be left on the marble for the briefest length of time and rinsed off thoroughly. A rust remover may be mixed into a kaolin or whiting poultice.

Polishing

Undamaged marble, after it has been cleaned, can be polished with a good quality silicone furniture polish which will give it an attractive sheen and some protection against water and weathering. A good quality commercial beeswax polish or home-made beeswax (see p. 44) can also be used. Use a minimum of polish and apply several well-worked-in coats rather than one thick application. Rub down well so that there is no sticky surface to attract dirt and dust. On a wide, flat surface such as the top of a wash-stand, a mechanical polisher with a thick polishing attachment will save a lot of effort. Work with care, as it may make grooves and scratches in the marble.

The traditional way to bring up a shine on marble is with a mild abrasive such as powdered chalk, fine grade whiting or putty powder rubbed in with a damp chamois leather. This will also remove very superficial staining. If you have used any of the bleaches or solvents mentioned above you will find that the surface of the marble has roughened and lost its shine. These patches are best treated in this traditional way. Small scratches and dents should also be smoothed away like this. However, it is a very time-consuming treatment for anything other than localised polishing. For the restoration of extensively damaged marble surfaces it is best so consult an expert.

Marble floors

Generally speaking, detergents and harsh abrasives should not be used on marble as they scratch the surface, take away the shine, and eventually cause discoloration. However, marble floors usually require radical treatment, and this means detergents. Clean marble floors in sections to avoid leaving water or detergent on for too long. Damp the section you are working on with a wet mop, sprinkle with detergent and then mop or scrub depending on how deeply ingrained the dirt is. Remove the dirty water immediately with clean water and a separate mop, before it has time to penetrate the marble. Stubborn stains can be drawn out by applying a poultice made of a thick paste of detergent into which you can mix an additional solvent or bleach if necessary. Be sure to remove all traces of the solvent when you have finished. A siliconised self-polishing floor wax will bring back the shine and help to protect the marble. Alternatively you can apply a transparent seal.

Mending marble

Broken sections of marble can be joined together again with an epoxy adhesive such as Araldite. The principles are exactly the same as for mending china (see p. 114), but you may well find you are having to keep very large and heavy pieces of stone clamped together while the join hardens. The principles of supporting and clamping remain the same but you will need to use stronger methods. For instance, two heavy old-fashioned door stops could be used to hold the pieces of a marble wash-stand top together. It is even more important than usual to give the adhesive time to dry—epoxy glues reach maximum efficiency after a week, or a little sooner if the object is baked. Disguise the join by polishing with a mild abrasive (see above).

Chips in marble and any groove still apparent when two pieces have been glued together can be filled with an epoxy putty (see p. 120) made by mixing an epoxy adhesive with as much kaolin or titanium dioxide as it will absorb. To achieve a shade as near the original as possible, add powdered colouring pigments or any powder resulting from abrading the marble itself. An alternative filler for coloured marble is plaster of Paris mixed with melted paraffin wax which can be coloured with candle dye from craft shops. Distinctive veining in the marble can be painted in afterwards. The dead white shade of white marble is achieved by mixing epoxy adhesive (Araldite) with titanium dioxide or talcum powder.

Missing sections of ornaments can be moulded from plaster of Paris, Barbola or coloured epoxy putty. Convincing results require artistic skill and practice. In some cases the replacement of missing sections will decrease the value of the subject.

Alabaster

Alabaster is very similar in composition to marble (see p. 140) and should be cleaned with one of the chemical solvents suitable for coloured marble. Alabaster is usually made into small decorative objects which are easily broken. It should be mended in the same way as china (see p. 114). If the alabaster is dead white add a little titanium dioxide to the epoxy adhesive which will help counteract its brownish tinge. Epoxy putty for filling white alabaster should also be made with titanium dioxide. Alabaster which is cream or brown will be matched best by a filler made of melted brown beeswax and plaster of Paris.

Soapstone

Soapstone is extremely soft, and makes a mark like soap when drawn across a sheet of glass. Finely ground soapstone is used as a mild abrasive called French chalk. Soapstone is usually found in the form of small carved ornaments.

Cleaning

Wash in mild soapy water; rinse and dry thoroughly. If heavily soiled, add a little detergent to the water or try the solvents suggested for marble (see p. 140).

Polishing

A sparing coat of silicone-based polish or good quality beeswax polish will restore the shine.

Mending

See marble (p. 142).

Jade

Several kinds of stone are designated as jade, so that apart from the usual green jade you may find it in shades of white, pink, yellow or blue. A useful guide in judging whether or not a stone is jade is its hardness, which makes it capable of scratching glass. It is usually found in the form of small carved ornaments.

Cleaning

Jade should simply be dusted with a soft cloth. Really dirty pieces may be washed in warm, mild soapsuds, carefully rinsed and thoroughly dried.

Mending

Broken jade can be glued together with an epoxy adhesive, using the methods given for china repair (see p. 114). Chips and cracks can be filled with epoxy putty. See the sections on marble and alabaster for ways of achieving a good colour match (p. 143).

Ivory

Ivory often turns up in the shape of small carvings. Eskimo carvings of narwhal or walrus tusks should be treated in the same way as elephant ivory. In addition ivory is used as a veneer (on piano keys, for example) or as part of intricate inlay work. Old ivory work is fragile and needs careful handling. Amateur repairs may detract from its value.

Cleaning

Ivory, which is a laminated material, may be damaged by water which gets between the layers and separates them. Wiping over with a soft cloth wrung out in warm soapy water, followed by thorough rinsing with a cloth wrung out in clean water and drying should be safe for all except the oldest and most fragile piece. Ingrained dirt should respond to a wipe with methylated spirit applied on a soft cloth or using a cotton baby bud to get into small carved crevices.

Bleaching

Ivory mellows naturally with age, the bright white of new piano keys being artificially produced by bleaching. Leaving a piano keyboard open so that it is exposed to the light will delay the yellowing process. If yellow piano keys trouble you, it may be possible to send the piano back to the factory to be refinished. Ivory can also be bleached with a paste made by mixing hydrogen peroxide with whiting. Do not let this paste get sloppy or it may penetrate the ivory and distort it. When the paste has dried brush it off and finish with a damp cloth. Dry thoroughly. Generally speaking ivory is best left to mellow with age.

Mending

Broken ivory can be glued together with an epoxy adhesive, mixing in a little titanium dioxide if necessary to whiten it. Use the method described for china (see p. 120).

Very frail ivory pieces which seem likely to splinter can be strengthened by impregnating them with paraffin wax. This will probably darken the ivory. The wax should be heated until it is liquid and the warmed object totally immersed in it. Leave for a few minutes, remove and wipe away any excess wax. Polish with a hot duster.

Polishing

Ivory can be polished with a fine abrasive such as whiting or pumice powder applied with a damp cloth or chamois leather.

Bone

Bone should be treated in the same way as ivory (see p. 145). Bone is often used for cutlery handles and these tend to come loose, especially if they have been mistakenly immersed in hot water over a period of time. The blades will need to be recemented into the handles. Remove the blade totally and clean out the hollow in the handle as thoroughly as possible with a skewer. Fill the cavity with melted natural resin, heat the tang of the blade over a flame until it is red hot and push it hard into the resin. Leave to cool.

Tortoiseshell and horn

Horn objects are usually made from cattle horn. Antlers are, of course, a form of horn. Tortoiseshell is made from turtle shells.

Cleaning

Wipe with a cloth wrung out in warm soapy water. A little detergent can be added if dirt is ingrained. Rinse with a cloth wrung out in warm water and dry thoroughly.

Polishing

Scratched horn and tortoiseshell can be buffed to a shine on a polishing wheel if you have one. Use a mild abrasive like whiting. Otherwise hand-polish with a mild abrasive powder such as rottenstone or whiting, applied with a damp cloth or a cloth coated with vaseline. A good quality wax polish or glycerine applied on a chamois leather will be sufficient to bring up a good shine on tortoiseshell or horn which already has a good smooth surface.

Mending

Mend as for china (see p. 114), using an epoxy adhesive such as Araldite, or a general purpose adhesive like Uhu.

Boulle work is a form of inlay using tortoiseshell with brass and ebony. Dirt can be wiped away with swabs of cotton wool wrung out in soapy water and the individual components cleaned by the best methods for each. Take care not to let water seep under the inlay and lift it up. It is best not to use solvent cleaners as these may dissolve the glues used to cement the components.

10

Common solvents and their applications

You may wish to treat items and materials not mentioned specifically in this book in which case you will find the following check-list of solvents and abrasives useful when choosing the best method of dealing with your particular problem. There is also a list of everyday stains and ways of removing them from most materials.

The solvents listed are generally available to the amateur. Nevertheless nearly all of them are potentially very dangerous. They should be used in well ventilated rooms or out in the open. Never use them anywhere near a naked flame (including a pilot light). When not in use they should be locked away in a cool place well out of the way of children and pets. They should always be clearly and correctly labelled. Most proprietary solvents contain one or other of the solvents listed below. Check manufacturers' labels to find out which one contains the substance most appropriate for the job you have to do (a chemist will usually explain the contents list). Check the label also for manufacturers' safety instructions.

Acetone Highly inflammable. Poisonous. Effects can be slowed down or halted by kerosene. Can be used on all natural and synthetic fibres except acetates. Found in proprietary nail polish remover. Fast solvent for varnishes/resins, paint, wax, epoxy adhesive before it sets.

Alcohol Inflammable. Some varieties poisonous. Effects can be slowed down or halted by turpentine or castor oil. See also methylated spirit, surgical spirit, white spirit. Solvent for oil, varnishes/resins, epoxy adhesive before it sets. Can also be used for cleaning glass.

Amyl acetate Highly inflammable. Dangerous fumes. Not for use on plastics or synthetics. Solvent for anything containing celluloid, *e.g.* cellulose based paints and lacquers.

Benzene Highly inflammable. Usually used on fabrics. Solvent for impact adhesives, *e.g.* Evostick, gums, resins/varnishes, phosphorous, sulphur, iodine. (*Benzol*, a proprietary mixture of benzene and toluene, has similar properties.)

Benzine (Petroleum ether) Liquid and vapour highly inflammable, not recommended. Solvent for impact adhesives *e.g.* Evostik, gums, fats, oil, resins/varnishes, phosphorous, sulphur, iodine.

Carbon bisulphide Highly inflammable. Dangerous fumes. Solvent for grease, oil, wax.

Chloroform Dangerous fumes. Solvent for wax including beeswax.

Chlorothene Not inflammable. Fumes less toxic than carbon tetrachloride. Increasingly used in household dry-cleaning fluids. Solvent for grease, oil, wax.

Ethyl acetate Inflammable. Dangerous fumes. Not for use on plastics or synthetics. Solvent for anything containing celluloid, *e.g.* cellulose-based paints and lacquers.

Methylated spirit (Wood alcohol+trace of pyridine) Inflammable. Poisonous. See Alcohol.

Petrol Highly inflammable liquid and vapour. Solvent for grease, oil, bitumen, mineral pitch.

Pyridine Inflammable. Poisonous. Solvent for grease, oil, old picture varnish.

Surgical spirit See Alcohol.

Turpentine Inflammable. Poisonous. Can be slowed down or halted by alcohol. Solvent for oil-based paints, resins/varnishes, waxes. Also used for making polishes.

Water/steam Solvent for non-synthetic glues and sugary substances.

White spirit (Commercial wood alcohol) Inflammable. Poisonous. A turpentine substitute but cannot be used in polishes. Solvent for oil-based paints, resins/varnishes, wax.

11

Common stains and their removal

All chemicals such as bleaches and solvents should be spot-tested on a hidden area of fabric before being applied to the whole article. Test for colour fastness by placing fabric on white blotting paper and patting with a damp cloth to see if colour transfers to blotting paper.

Adhesive and tape marks on upholstery, china, etc
Use a proprietary cleaning fluid or acetone. If these are unsuccessful look at the list of solvents on p. 147).

Alcohol
On wood see p. 10.
On marble see p. 140.
On fabrics mop up as soon as possible with absorbent paper applying plenty of pressure. Do not rub the stain and spread it. White fabrics can be bleached with a mild bleach such as 5 per cent hydrogen peroxide. Soak colourfast fabrics in a solution of mild liquid detergent plus 1 level tablespoonful of borax for every half litre of water. Non-colourfast fabrics can be gently sponged with the same solution. Alternatively sponge the stain with a solution of 1 part white spirit to 2 parts water.

Alcohol is found in many cosmetics and perfumes as well as in drinks.

Blood
Fresh stains on colourfast materials should be *immediately* rinsed out in several changes of cold water then washed in warm soapy water. Non-colourfast materials should be sponged with cold water then ‘washed’ with a cloth wrung out in detergent solution and ‘rinsed’ with a cloth wrung out in clean water. A ‘poultice’ of starch or corn-

flour mixed to a stiff paste with cold water can also be applied to the marked fabric. Allow the 'poultice' to dry and absorb the stain then brush off. This is a particularly useful technique on delicate fabrics and can be used on other fresh stains.

Old or persistent bloodstains can be dabbed with a little ammonia and then washed or sponged. Old bloodstains may also become less noticeable if soaked in, or sponged with, a mild solution of bleach. Enzyme detergents can be used on fabric which is not delicate. A specialist dry-cleaner may treat bloodstains effectively.

Coffee and tea

Fresh stains on colourfast materials should be rinsed out immediately in several changes of cold water. Sponge non-colourfast materials with cold water, then sponge with mild detergent solution and 'rinse' by sponging with warm water. Colourfast materials can be laundered in the usual way. If milk or cream causes grease marks see Grease and oil. A mild bleach may remove old or stubborn stains. Enzyme detergent can be used on fabrics which are washable and not delicate.

Dye

If a cleaning method causes dye to run try sponging the area to which the colour has spread with methylated spirit plus a few drops of ammonia or with chlorine bleach if the material can take it. 'Rinse' by sponging with distilled water.

Glue (see also Adhesive)

Most woodwork shops sell proprietary glue solvents. Many old glues dissolve in hot water. Methylated spirit may soften epoxy adhesives. See also the list of solvents on p. 147.

Grease and oil

On books and papers see p. 64.
On leather see p. 90.

On fabric dampen round the stain with water to prevent it spreading, then treat with an appropriate solvent (see solvents p. 147), or with a proprietary dry-cleaning product. Alternatively use a spray dry-cleaner which sprays a grease-absorbing powder on to the stain. Brush off when dry. Delicate fabrics can be sprinkled with a layer of talcum powder or Fuller's Earth which is brushed off when it has absorbed the grease. Most grease and oil stains can be removed by expert dry-cleaners.

Fruit stains

Rinse colourfast materials in cold water. Sponge non-colourfast materials with cold water. Do not use soap and water on fresh stains before you have rinsed them as this will set them. For the same reason do not iron before you have removed as much of the stain as possible. After rinsing, launder as usual. On non-colourfast materials sponge with a mild detergent solution and 'rinse' by sponging with warm water. An enzyme detergent can be used on washable fabrics.

Inks

On wood see p. 9.

On old fabrics ink stains are usually from fountain pen ink, which was made with different ingredients at different times. One of the following methods may be effective:

Proprietary ink remover, available from chemists;
Glycerine, applied to the stain to loosen it then washed or sponged and rinsed well;
Ammonia applied directly to the stain and then washed or sponged out;
A mild bleach which should be rinsed out after use;
On white fabrics sprinkle the stain with salt, rub with half a cut lemon, leave for an hour or so then rinse or sponge off;
Equal parts of methylated spirit and water sponged on the stain and then washed or sponged off;

Ball point pen marks may respond to a proprietary remover. Otherwise try sponging with neat methylated spirit, wash or sponge off and rinse. Oil of Eucalyptus rubbed into ballpoint stains sometimes loosens them. Launder as usual.

Mildew

Almost impossible to remove but may be less noticeable if bleached. Use a mild bleach on delicate fabrics. Chlorine bleach can be used on white linens and cottons. Rinse well. Methylated spirit sometimes works as a spot remover.

Paint and varnish

Fresh paint should be laundered immediately. Old paint should be treated with an appropriate solvent (p. 147), and laundered thoroughly while the paint is still moist from the solvent.

Rust and iron mould

Most common on old upholstery in contact with rusting tacks and nails. Sprinkle with salt and rub with a cut lemon or sprinkle with salt and lemon juice and leave to dry in the sun. You may be able to buy a proprietary rust remover from the chemist. Strong chemicals should not be used on delicate fabrics.

Bleach may be used to remove rust marks from colourfast fabrics. Soak or sponge on. Rinse.

Wax

On paper and books see p. 65.

On fabric scrape off the excess with a knife. Place the fabric between sheets of clean white blotting paper (or similar absorbent paper). Iron with a warm iron – the paper will absorb the wax as it melts. Replace the paper as soon as it absorbs any wax. Launder or dry-clean.

Wine See Alcohol

Book list

Berger, Robert, *All about Antiquing and Restoring Furniture*. Hawthorn Books, Inc. New York.

Burdett, *The Craft of Bookbinding*. David and Charles Ltd, Devon.

Johnstone, James B. and Sunset Editorial Staff, *Furniture Upholstery and Repair*. Lane Books, California.

Kinney, Ralph, *The Complete Book of Furniture Repair and Refinishing*. Charles Scribner's Sons, New York.

Pearsall, Ronald, *Collecting and Restoring Scientific Instruments*. David and Charles Ltd, Devon.

Pearsall, Ronald, *Collecting Mechanical Antiques*. David and Charles Ltd, Devon.

Plenderleith, H. J. and Werner, A. E. A., *Conservation of Antiques and Works of Art: Treatment, Repair and Restoration*. Oxford University Press, London.

Rodd, John, *Repairing and Restoring Antique Furniture*, David and Charles Ltd, Devon.

Savage, George, *The Art and Antique Restorers' Handbook*. Barrie and Rockliff.

Smith, Eric, *Repairing Antique Clocks*. David and Charles Ltd, Devon.

Toller, Jane, *Discovering Antiques*. David and Charles Ltd, Devon.

Toller, Jane, *Treen*. David and Charles Ltd, Devon.

Teach Yourself Books

Bainbridge, C. G., *Welding*.

Fairfield, Del, *Enamelling*.

Fairfield, Del, *Lapidary*.

Hayward, Charles, *Carpentry*.

Howard, T. O. and Oughton, F., *Joinery*.

Oughton, Frederick, *Creative Crafts*.

Metric conversion table

Equivalents shown below are only approximate

1 in = 2.54 cm	21 in = 53 cm
2 in = 5 cm	22 in = 55 cm
3 in = 7½ cm	23 in = 58 cm
4 in = 10 cm	24 in = 60 cm
5 in = 13 cm	25 in = 63 cm
6 in = 15 cm	26 in = 65 cm
7 in = 18 cm	27 in = 68 cm
8 in = 20 cm	28 in = 71 cm
9 in = 23 cm	29 in = 73 cm
10 in = 26 cm	30 in = 76 cm
11 in = 28 cm	31 in = 78 cm
12 in = 30 cm	32 in = 81 cm
13 in = 33 cm	33 in = 83 cm
14 in = 35 cm	34 in = 86 cm
15 in = 38 cm	35 in = 88 cm
16 in = 40 cm	36 in = 91½ cm
17 in = 43 cm	37 in = 93 cm
18 in = 45 cm	38 in = 96 cm
19 in = 48 cm	39 in = 99 cm
20 in = 50 cm	40 in = 101½ cm

Index

TEACH YOURSELF BOOKS

HOUSE REPAIRS

Tony Wilkins

Buying a house is probably the biggest financial outlay you will ever make. However, if this asset is not to become a liability, a continuous programme of repair and maintenance is of great importance. Neglect soon leads to an increasing number of problems and general deterioration of the fabric.

The problems you meet will, of course, vary according to the type of property you have but, whatever they are, you can make considerable financial savings by dealing with them yourself.

This book will both help you to identify trouble spots and provide you with the knowledge to enable you to do a good job. A summary of the problems you might find, both inside and outside the house, is followed by a reference section of advice on how to tackle them. Topics covered include the roof, doors, windows, walls, damp, house surrounds, floors, ceilings and drainage.

Tony Wilkins is Editor of DIY magazine.

UNITED KINGDOM	£1·25
AUSTRALIA	$3·95*
NEW ZEALAND	$3·95
CANADA	$4·25

*recommended but not obligatory

ISBN 0 340 22242 5